THE
BAD BOY FORMULA

Change Your Mindset and Become
the Man Women Can't Ignore

LOGAN CREED

Copyright © 2025 – All rights reserved.

No part of this publication may be reproduced, distributed, or transmitted in any form or by any means, whether electronic, mechanical, photocopying, recording, or otherwise, without the prior written permission of the publisher, except in the case of brief quotations used in reviews, articles, or scholarly works. All photographs and artwork were created by the author using the most recent digital design methods, including advanced image-generation software.

While every effort has been made to ensure accuracy, the author and publisher make no representations or warranties regarding the completeness or accuracy of the contents of this book and specifically disclaim any implied warranties of merchantability or fitness for a particular purpose.

Table of Contents

The Myth of the Bad Boy 5
The Men in the Age of Noise 11
    The Silent Crisis of Success 13
    The Overstimulated Male 17
    The Rediscovery of Silence 21
    The Nice Guy Epidemic 25
    Rebuilding Honesty and Edge 29
    Rebellion Against Weakness 33
    From Reaction to Leadership 36

The Bad Boy Formula 39
    F – Fearless Mindset (Concept) 40
    F – Fearless Mindset (Application) 44
    O – Own Your Energy (Concept) 47
    O – Own Your Energy (Application) 51
    R – Rules of Rebellion (Concept) 55
    R – Rules of Rebellion (Application) 59
    M – Magnetic Habits (Concept) 63
    M – Magnetic Habits (Application) 67
    U – Unshakable Standards (Concept) 71
    U – Unshakable Standards (Application) 75
    L – Leadership (Concept) 79
    L – Leadership (Application) 83
    A – Attraction (Concept) 87
    A – Attraction (Application) 90

The Inner Empire: Self-Mastery 94
The Discipline Code (Concept) 96
The Discipline Code (Application) 99
The Inner Voice (Concept) 102
The Inner Voice (Application) 106
The Warrior and the Monk 109
Purpose Over Pleasure 112
Mastery in Relationships 115
Polarity and Power 117
Charisma and Connection 120
Boundaries in Love 124
Boundaries in Love 127
The Art of Attraction in Practice 131
The Magnetic Approach 134
The Deep Connection Blueprint 137
Sustaining Desire 140
Become the Gravity 143

The Myth of the Bad Boy

They call him dangerous. They say he's trouble, unpredictable, maybe even toxic. But what they don't understand is that the man they're describing isn't the villain — he's the reflection of what every man secretly wants to be: **free.**

The "bad boy" has become a cultural ghost. We see him in movies, in music, in the men women whisper about when they think no one is listening. He's not good because he's perfect. He's good because he's **real** — a man who lives by instinct instead of approval. Society warns against him, but that only makes him magnetic. He's the storm that moves through a world of still air.

The modern world has twisted his image. It sells rebellion in cologne ads and leather jackets, but it hides the truth that rebellion doesn't come from what you wear — it comes from what you **refuse** to obey. The "bad boy" isn't bad because he breaks rules. He's bad because he doesn't need permission.

And that's what terrifies people.

Because if you don't need permission, you can't be controlled. You stop seeking validation. You stop performing. You start walking differently, speaking slower, standing taller — because your movements belong to you again. The world will label you arrogant when you stop apologizing for your own presence. But confidence isn't arrogance. It's alignment. It's knowing that your time, your energy, and your attention are sacred — and acting like it.

The problem is, men today have been raised to disconnect from that energy. We're told to play nice. To be liked. To never offend. And somewhere between politeness and performance, we forgot how to feel powerful. We became agreeable. Predictable. Safe. But attraction doesn't live in safety — it lives in tension. Women don't crave danger; they crave direction. They don't want chaos; they want presence.

That's the real misunderstanding.

The "bad boy" isn't cruel — he's **centered.** He doesn't chase, not because he's playing games, but because his attention is earned. He can love deeply, but never desperately. He can be kind, but never submissive. He's not out to control anyone — he simply won't be controlled.

You can see it when he walks into a room. He doesn't rush to fill the silence. He owns it. His calmness is louder than other men's noise. He's not in competition because he's already chosen himself. That's what women feel — not his looks, not his clothes, not his mystery. They feel his **freedom.**

Freedom is the most magnetic energy on earth. When a man is free inside, everyone around him senses it. His movements are unforced. His words have weight. His eyes don't dart around seeking approval — they rest, steady, aware. He doesn't need to dominate others to prove power. His calm *is* power.

That's the essence this book is built on. The "Bad Boy Formula" isn't about pretending to be something you're not. It's about stripping away everything you were told to be until what's left is the man you always were — honest, strong, grounded, dangerous in his peace.

You'll notice something else about the real "bad boy": he doesn't call himself one. The label comes from those who can't categorize him. Society has trained people to fear what it can't domesticate. So when a man stands in quiet confidence, he's misunderstood. When he refuses to follow, he's accused of arrogance. When he says no, he's labeled selfish. But underneath those labels is the truth: **independence is intimidating** to those who've never tasted it.

So the world tells men to play smaller, to lower their volume, to become softer versions of themselves. And then it wonders why women lose interest, why men feel lost, and why attraction feels like a ghost of something we used to know.

Here's the secret: the "bad boy" never disappeared. He just got buried under comfort, conformity, and digital noise. This book is about digging him out — not to become reckless, but to become **real.** To live with purpose. To act with direction. To reclaim the instinct that once made men magnetic: presence.

Because presence is the ultimate rebellion. It's the thing the modern world can't sell, replicate, or fake. When you're present, you're untouchable. You stop chasing things that weaken you. You start building a life that draws everything you want naturally.

That's what this journey is about — rediscovering your natural dominance, your quiet power, and your ability to move through the world with calm authority.

The "bad boy" isn't an act. He's an awakening. He's not here to prove anything — he's here to **remember.**

The Instinct of Presence

She won't be able to explain it. She'll say he had "something about him." A look. A vibe. Energy. But what she's really feeling — before words, before logic — is **presence**.

And it's not just attraction. It's instinct. It's not something she chooses. It's something she responds to.

Women are not drawn to noise. They're drawn to **centered gravity** — the man who knows exactly where he stands and doesn't flinch. When a man leads himself without hesitation, it triggers something ancient in her. A signal that says: *he can handle the world, and he can handle me.*

It has nothing to do with dominance in the loud, performative way. It's not about raising your voice or puffing your chest. That's posturing, and she sees through it instantly. She's not looking for a man who tries to impress. She's looking for a man who doesn't need to.

Because that man — the one who is quietly grounded — makes her feel something rare: **safe and alive at the same time.**

That's where attraction really lives. Not in looks, not in money, not even in conversation. It lives in how you make her feel in your presence. And here's the truth most men never hear: if you don't trust your own energy, neither will she.

Masculine presence doesn't mean being stoic to the point of coldness. It means being **unshaken**. You can smile. You can tease. You can open up. But underneath it all, she needs to feel that you won't be pulled off-center by her emotions — or your own. That no matter how the energy shifts, **you remain the anchor.**

Because when a woman is near a truly grounded man, something unlocks in her. Her nervous system softens. Her walls lower. She stops performing and starts responding. That response isn't logical. It's biological.

For generations, women survived by sensing danger, leadership, and strength not in words — but in **vibe**. In cues. In how a man carries himself, how he breathes, how his gaze holds or falters. Her instincts are designed to read the room faster than you can think. She doesn't need to know your resume. She needs to know if she can **relax in your frame.**

When you lead yourself — your emotions, your decisions, your reactions — you naturally lead her too. That's what makes a woman melt: not control, but **direction.**

And that's the quiet magic of masculine presence. It's subtle, but powerful. It's the eye contact that doesn't waver. The slow, unrushed breath. The pause between your words — not because you're unsure, but because you're not in a hurry to be understood. Because you already understand yourself.

That's leadership. Not barking orders or making demands. But creating a rhythm — a gravitational pull — that brings everything and everyone into orbit. That's what she's responding to when she says, "There was something about him." It's not about arrogance. Arrogance is loud. Arrogance needs attention.

Presence doesn't need anything. Presence *gives*.

It gives direction. It gives stability. It gives **space** for the feminine to express without collapsing the masculine. And in that space, desire grows. Because polarity — that electric spark between the masculine and feminine — isn't about being "better." It's about being **opposite** in a way that fits. She brings the flow. You bring the structure. She brings the emotion. You bring the container. She brings the storm. You bring the calm.

Not because she can't handle herself. But because when a man meets her with grounded energy, she finally doesn't *have* to.

That's the leadership she's craving. Not control. Not ego. But direction.

And when you give it — not through dominance, but through inner clarity — her instincts recognize it instantly. That's why she can feel it across the room. That's why the "bad boy" is unforgettable. Not because of the trouble he brings, but because of the **presence he holds**. Because in a world of men who hesitate, who shrink, who doubt themselves into silence… He doesn't. He leads. And she follows not because he forces her to — but because she **wants to.**

The Return

You don't need to become someone new. You just need to remember. Underneath the layers of hesitation, politeness, self-doubt, and performance… is a man who was built for presence. Built for direction. Built to lead himself first — and then everything around him.

That man still lives in you.

You've seen glimpses of him. In moments where you spoke without second-guessing. In the way you looked at her before you knew what to say. In the days where you moved through the world with purpose, and everything seemed to fall into rhythm around you. That wasn't a fluke. That was you, before the noise. Before the softness of society dulled your sharpness. Before the world asked you to apologize for being a man.

The "bad boy" everyone talks about isn't a character you put on. He's what you become when you strip away everything that's not *you*.

This book isn't about learning lines or playing roles. It's about returning to your center — the place where attraction isn't forced, and confidence isn't performed. Where you speak less, mean more, and stop chasing things that should naturally be drawn to you.

That version of you is not out of reach. He's been buried, not broken. Forgotten, not gone. And the process of becoming magnetic — truly magnetic — begins by coming back to yourself. Back to your standards. Back to your energy. Back to your presence. That's what this book will give you. Not another mask. Not another performance. But your edge. Your fire. Your power — without needing to raise your voice to feel it. And yes — women will notice. Because when you lead yourself, they feel it. When you stop needing, they lean in. When you return to who you really are… they *remember* who they are, too.

But that part comes later. Because to understand how to become magnetic, we first need to understand what's dulled our edge.

The Men in the Age of Noise

Masculinity hasn't disappeared but it's definitely been diluted.

Over the last few decades, something subtle but serious has taken place. The instinct that once drove men to challenge themselves, to take risks, to build, protect, and lead, has been buried under layers of comfort, convenience, and social conditioning.

Men were told to be more agreeable. To behave. To soften up. At first, it seemed like harmless advice. Society said it wanted kinder, more emotionally intelligent men. And sure — emotional depth is important. But that wasn't all that changed. Alongside the call for empathy came an unspoken pressure: lose your edge, keep your head down, don't make waves.

And men listened. We traded danger for stability. Direction for safety. Presence for passivity.

Today, the modern man is more "comfortable" than ever — but also more restless, more distracted, and more unsure of his role in the world. He might have a decent job, a dating app or two, a gym membership. On paper, things look fine. But deep down, something feels off. The edge is missing. The fire is gone.

That fire was the instinct for challenge. Not drama, not aggression — challenge. The desire to push yourself into discomfort, to do something difficult just because it tests you. That part of masculinity has always been inconvenient for society. It's harder to manage men who think for themselves. It's easier to sell to men who are bored, overstimulated, and docile.

So the culture gave you alternatives: cheap dopamine, endless entertainment, comfort in every direction. And in return, it took something from you — your hunger.

Men stopped pursuing depth. Instead, they started performing. Trying to be liked. Trying to avoid offense. Trying to be "good" by someone else's definition.

But here's the truth: when men lose their connection to discomfort, they lose their connection to themselves. Because masculinity isn't born in comfort. It's born in struggle, in structure, in self-control. In being able to do hard things without needing applause for it.

This isn't about going backwards or romanticizing the past. It's about recognizing that we've created a version of masculinity that's been sterilized. And the results speak for themselves: fewer strong relationships, fewer grounded men, and an entire generation wondering why they feel numb even though life is technically "easy."

Comfort without direction leads nowhere. The world told you to be safe, but forgot to remind you to be strong. And without strength — physical, mental, emotional — men drift.

You're not broken. You've just been conditioned out of your nature. And now it's time to reverse that. Not by becoming a caricature of masculinity. Not by chasing extremes. But by rebuilding the foundation — your mindset, your values, your instincts. That's where this book starts. With the truth that the world won't give you your edge back. You have to take it.

The Silent Crisis of Success

He has the job. The car. The apartment that overlooks a city built on ambition. On paper, he's everything the world told him to become. Yet when he wakes up, there's a quiet heaviness behind his ribs — a question that doesn't go away: *Is this it?*

It's not that he's ungrateful. It's that he's unfulfilled. Somewhere between building a résumé and building a life, something essential went missing. He became efficient, but not alive. Accomplished, but not anchored. Successful, but strangely hollow.

This is the silent crisis of the modern man — the man who appears to be winning yet feels like he's drifting. He's achieved what he was told would bring him confidence, but it hasn't touched his soul. He's surrounded by comfort yet haunted by restlessness. The more he achieves, the less he feels. Because no matter how much he accumulates, the mirror never lies: he doesn't recognize the man looking back.

What he's missing isn't motivation — it's meaning. He's been conditioned to chase milestones, not mastery. To measure progress by metrics, not presence. To be productive, not powerful. Society congratulated him for climbing ladders but never asked if the ladder was leaning against the right wall.

He was told that success would make him whole. But success without soul doesn't satisfy — it sedates.

The modern world praises men for their output, but not their depth. You can hit targets, close deals, and post highlights online, yet still feel invisible to yourself. You've been taught to build an image — but not an identity. To chase applause — but not alignment. You're surrounded by noise, yet starving for silence.

It's easy to hide behind achievements. They give the illusion of strength. But real strength isn't in what you show; it's in what you can sit with when the applause fades. It's in the nights where you lie awake, realizing you've built everything except the feeling of being alive.

That's the moment every man meets himself — when the external trophies stop numbing the internal emptiness. When success feels more like armor than freedom. When he realizes that performance can't replace presence. And this isn't weakness. It's awakening.

Because beneath the metrics and milestones lies a deeper hunger — the desire to feel *real again*. To move through life with fire, not fatigue. To look in the mirror and see a man who doesn't just *do*, but *is*. Who doesn't just achieve, but *feels power flowing through him*.

The truth is, many men were never taught how to win *internally*. They were taught how to perform — for teachers, bosses, parents, women, algorithms. Every victory was a transaction: approval in exchange for authenticity. But the soul doesn't thrive on transactions. It thrives on truth.

So when that truth is buried under pressure and pretense, a quiet depression begins. The man who's always "doing fine" begins to fade from his own life. He smiles at dinners, checks boxes at work, and scrolls through distractions at night — all to avoid the silence that might reveal how disconnected he's become.

And yet, that silence is exactly where the cure lives.

Because when you finally stop performing long enough to feel the emptiness, you're no longer lost — you're found. You're finally facing what's real. The hollow feeling isn't failure. It's a signal — the call back to your edge. The whisper that says, *this isn't your peak, it's your pause*.

That's where the rebuilding begins.

The men who come back to life aren't the ones who chase more — they're the ones who strip away what doesn't matter. They stop confusing busyness for purpose. They stop living by other people's definitions of success. They stop performing for validation that can't fill them.

And as they peel back the layers of noise, something shifts. Focus returns. Desire sharpens. Direction reappears.

Because true fulfillment doesn't come from adding more — it comes from aligning more deeply. You don't need to build a bigger life; you need to build a truer one.

That's when a man's energy changes. His eyes stop darting around searching for approval. His movements slow down. His words become deliberate. He stops chasing excitement and starts creating meaning. Women feel it immediately — that grounded steadiness that says, *I know who I am again.*

This is what the world doesn't understand about masculine fulfillment. It's not found in outcomes. It's found in ownership. Ownership of your energy. Ownership of your direction. Ownership of your time, attention, and standards.

A man who owns himself doesn't need to prove himself. He can walk into a room with quiet confidence because he's not carrying the weight of pretending anymore. His worth isn't conditional. His success isn't decoration — it's expression. Everything he builds now comes from a full heart, not a hollow chase.

And that shift — from hollow achievement to grounded purpose — is what makes a man magnetic again. Because magnetism isn't about being noticed. It's about being *felt*. You can't fake it, and you can't buy it. It comes from the peace that only arrives when your inner world matches your outer one. That's why the "bad boy" — the man who lives from truth, not approval — seems so alive. He may not have it all figured out, but he's *in rhythm*. His power isn't perfect; it's real. And that realness is rarer than ever.

This crisis of success is the turning point — the crack in the armor that lets light back in. It's the moment you realize that no amount of validation will replace the feeling of being connected to yourself. And when that realization hits, you can't go back to living on autopilot.

You start craving something deeper: clarity, challenge, silence — the ingredients of presence. And presence is where your edge returns. Because the man who rediscovers his edge doesn't need to chase meaning anymore. He *becomes* it. His life starts to feel like his again — raw, intentional, magnetic. And that's where we go next. To reclaim the edge, we must first face the enemy that's dulling it — the overstimulation that numbs a man's hunger before it even begins.

The Overstimulated Male

If the modern man feels hollow, it's not because he lacks access to pleasure. It's because he has too much of it.

Everywhere he turns, something is trying to capture his attention, to feed him a hit of excitement, to make him feel something — anything — for just a second. He wakes up to a glowing screen that starts whispering before his thoughts can even form. Notifications, messages, reels, headlines — each one engineered to flood his brain with dopamine, that tiny chemical reward that once drove our ancestors to hunt, build, and survive. Now it drives us to scroll, to consume, to distract ourselves from the silence that might actually save us.

He doesn't realize it, but his nervous system is constantly on a leash. Every swipe, every click, every new video, every new face on a dating app — it's all a jolt. A false spark. It's not passion. It's stimulation. And the more stimulation he takes in, the duller his instincts become. His attention fragments. His focus fades. He becomes a man who reacts instead of leads.

In a world where everything is available instantly, desire itself has lost its weight. The chase, the hunger, the slow burn that once made men feel alive has been replaced by instant gratification. He no longer works for reward; he taps for it. He doesn't court patience; he avoids it. The modern man has traded intensity for immediacy, not realizing that the former builds him while the latter bleeds him dry.

This is what overstimulation does — it hijacks your masculine energy at its core. Masculinity thrives on focus, direction, and delayed gratification. It's built through tension — the kind that refines desire into discipline. But dopamine on demand erases that tension. It gives you the illusion of satisfaction without any of the depth. You start confusing arousal with desire, distraction with excitement, busyness with purpose. You feel like you're living, but you're only reacting.

And so the modern man drifts. He consumes images of the life he wants instead of building it. He watches others move with purpose while he scrolls for another shot of motivation to replace the one that faded an hour ago. He tells himself he's "taking a break," but the truth is he's escaping — from stillness, from boredom, from the raw space where real power grows.

Because real desire — the kind that drives you to build, to pursue, to lead — can only survive in silence. It needs friction. It needs space to breathe. When every spare moment is filled with noise, there's no room left for that hunger to rise. The man who floods his senses forgets how to feel deeply. He becomes addicted to novelty, incapable of depth. Every new thing loses its taste faster than the last, leaving him chasing stimulation instead of satisfaction.

This is why attention has become the new currency of power — not just in business or media, but in masculinity itself. The man who can control his attention controls his energy. And the man who controls his energy controls his life. But most men have given that power away. They've let their focus be auctioned off to whoever shouts the loudest.

Porn is a perfect example. It promises pleasure, but what it delivers is emptiness. It gives you a flood of dopamine without the depth of connection, without the challenge of pursuit, without the satisfaction of presence. It's the ultimate illusion of conquest — an experience that tricks your biology into thinking you've lived something powerful, when in truth you've only escaped into pixels. Over time, it dulls your instincts. It rewires your attraction to instant highs and erases your ability to find meaning in the slow unfolding of real intimacy. The screen becomes your lover, and your confidence slowly erodes.

Social media does the same thing on a broader scale. Every scroll tells you who you should be, what you should have, who you should date, and how you should live. It sells you idealized versions of yourself and then punishes you for not living up to them. You end up performing for strangers while losing touch with the man you actually are. The noise doesn't just distract you; it conditions you to need it. Without it, you feel uneasy, like silence has become threatening. That's how you know the addiction has set in — when stillness feels unbearable.

This is the quiet tragedy of overstimulation: it doesn't destroy men all at once. It dissolves them slowly. Every moment of mindless consumption chips away at clarity. Every unexamined impulse makes him weaker, not in strength, but in will. The mind that once directed energy outward — to build, to conquer, to protect — now spends that same energy refreshing feeds, chasing notifications, seeking stimulation that never ends. And beneath it all, the fire that once burned in him starts to dim.

The most dangerous kind of weakness is the one that hides behind activity. He looks busy, engaged, connected. But if you strip away the screens and the distractions, there's nothing steady underneath. The overstimulated man is restless because he's out of rhythm with himself. His attention is scattered, his body anxious, his desire confused. He no longer knows what he truly wants because he's never given himself enough silence to hear the answer.

Reclaiming focus is not about quitting technology or renouncing pleasure. It's about reconditioning your nervous system to crave depth over dopamine. It's about choosing friction again — the friction of effort, of delayed gratification, of not knowing what comes next and being okay with it. Because that's where masculinity lives: in the space between craving and control.

When you stop reaching for constant stimulation, you rediscover something ancient — stillness. And stillness is where presence begins. It's where you start to feel your own power again, not as excitement, but as gravity. The man who can sit in silence without needing escape becomes dangerous in the best way. His energy consolidates. His gaze steadies. His movements slow down until every gesture carries weight.

He doesn't need the world to keep him entertained anymore. He becomes the source of his own stimulation — the generator of his own fire. And when a man reaches that point, the world begins to respond to him differently. Opportunities appear where they didn't before. People listen when he speaks. Women sense his grounded energy and feel safe in it. He's no longer broadcasting noise; he's radiating presence.

But that transformation can only begin when he's willing to step away from the constant hum of distraction and return to the ancient skill every powerful man once mastered: solitude. Because in solitude, you stop reacting and start remembering. You remember what you want, what you value, and who you are when the noise fades.

And that's where we go next — into the rediscovery of silence. Because before a man can lead others, he must learn to lead himself back into stillness.

The Rediscovery of Silence

There comes a point when the noise becomes unbearable. Not because it's too loud — but because it's endless. The mind, overstimulated and exhausted, starts to crave something it once feared: quiet. At first, that quiet feels like a void. It feels empty, uncertain, almost threatening. But if you stay in it long enough, something subtle begins to shift. The emptiness turns into space. And within that space, you start to hear again — not the world, but yourself.

Stillness has become the rarest luxury of the modern age. Most men avoid it because it forces them to face the truth that no amount of external success can silence inner chaos. Yet stillness is exactly what restores order. In silence, distractions fall away. In solitude, masks come off. And in boredom — that forgotten teacher — your instincts begin to stretch and wake, remembering what it means to create from hunger instead of habit.

You can tell when a man has reconnected with silence. His energy changes. His presence thickens, like the air around him carries more gravity. He doesn't fidget or fill every pause with noise. He speaks less, but when he does, his words have weight. He looks at you and you feel it — not because he's trying to project confidence, but because his focus is undivided. He's not scattered between tabs, screens, or notifications. He's *there*. Fully.

That kind of presence can't be faked. It comes only from solitude. From choosing, deliberately, to step away from constant stimulation and face your own restlessness. It's not comfortable at first. The mind rebels. It demands distraction, comfort, relief. But once you stop running from the discomfort of silence, you discover that it's not emptiness you've been afraid of — it's power.

Because in silence, all the false signals disappear. You stop performing. You stop comparing. You stop seeking validation from the outside world.

And when all that noise fades, you begin to sense something ancient stirring underneath — the quiet hum of your own strength. The masculine edge isn't built in chaos; it's sharpened in calm.

The world taught men to equate energy with movement — to always be busy, always be chasing, always be producing. But real power moves slower. It doesn't rush. It waits, observes, decides. That's why silence is so potent: it slows you down until your actions align with intention. You stop reacting impulsively. You start choosing deliberately. Your life starts to feel less like noise and more like rhythm.

And women notice. They might not be able to explain it logically, but they feel it instinctively. A man who has mastered stillness carries a different frequency. He's not searching for stimulation because he's already full. His presence doesn't reach outward — it pulls inward. It draws people, especially women, into his orbit. Because the feminine doesn't want a man who is constantly chasing motion; she wants a man who *anchors* it.

That's what stillness does — it creates a gravitational field. When you stand in your own quiet power, you become a mirror. Her emotions, her energy, her movement — they all find balance in your calm. She feels safe to express herself because you won't be swept away by her storm. You're not trying to control it; you're simply unmoved by it. And that steadiness, that unshakable frame, is what she interprets as strength.

It's not the silence of detachment. It's the silence of presence — the kind that listens deeply, notices details, and acts with precision. When you've spent time alone in stillness, you stop fearing emotional intensity. You stop needing to fix or escape it. You've already faced your own chaos in solitude, so hers doesn't intimidate you. You simply hold it, with the quiet confidence of a man who trusts his own center.

This is why solitude isn't isolation — it's integration. You're not running from the world. You're refining your relationship with it. You're learning to move without being moved, to engage without being consumed. And when you return to the world after periods of silence, you notice something incredible: your senses are sharper. Colors seem richer. Conversations carry more depth. You're no longer numbed by overstimulation; you're alive to every detail.

Even boredom becomes a gift. Boredom is the friction that forces creativity to return. When you stop giving your mind constant entertainment, it starts to reach deeper. It begins to imagine, to build, to create. This is where direction and purpose come from — not from pressure, but from space. Great ideas don't emerge in chaos; they rise from quiet minds that know how to wait.

Every man needs this silence, not as an escape but as a ritual. To unplug from the noise long enough to remember who he is without the world's reflection. To spend time alone not as punishment, but as practice. Stillness doesn't make you soft — it makes you precise. The warrior who can sit in calm before battle will always move with more clarity than the one who can't sit still.

That's what the modern world has forgotten. It glorifies the loud, the constant, the visible. But the most dangerous men in history — the ones who led, built, and changed everything — all shared one thing: they spent time alone. In that solitude, they met themselves without distraction, without audience, without validation. And when they returned, their words carried the kind of certainty that can't be taught — only found.

You can feel that same transformation beginning the moment you stop reaching for your phone and let silence wash over you. At first, it will feel awkward. Then, slowly, it will start to feel sacred. You'll begin to crave it the way you once craved stimulation. Because silence doesn't drain you — it restores you. It brings your power back home.

And the next time you walk into a room, you won't need to speak loudly or move quickly. Your presence will do the talking. She'll feel it before she even understands it — that grounded, quiet certainty that separates men who are performers from men who are anchored. She won't be drawn to you because you're loud or impressive. She'll be drawn to you because your energy says, *I'm here, and I'm not moving.*

That's the rediscovery of silence — not the absence of sound, but the presence of self. It's the foundation of true power, the soil from which focus, confidence, and magnetism all grow. And once a man has tasted that kind of power, he stops living for attention and starts living from intention. He no longer seeks validation. He embodies direction. And that shift — from performing to leading — is where the next evolution begins.

The Nice Guy Epidemic

Silence teaches a man to be whole on his own. But most men were never taught that lesson. They were raised instead to seek approval — to be liked, to be agreeable, to never disrupt the room. Somewhere along the way, kindness was confused with compliance, and confidence was replaced with accommodation. The result is what we now see everywhere: the epidemic of the "Nice Guy."

On the surface, he seems perfect. He listens. He smiles. He never argues. He texts back quickly, compliments often, and apologizes even when he's done nothing wrong. He lives to please. But beneath the politeness is something fragile — a quiet desperation to be accepted. The Nice Guy doesn't act out of self-assurance. He acts out of fear: fear of rejection, fear of conflict, fear of not being enough.

He believes that if he's endlessly kind, people will finally see his worth. But approval-seeking is not connection — it's negotiation. It's a subtle trade: "I'll make you comfortable if you'll give me validation." Every smile hides a silent contract. And the problem with that contract is that it kills respect before it ever creates attraction.

Women sense this instinctively. They might appreciate the attention, but they don't *feel* the man behind it. His energy is soft, hesitant, diluted. He wants to be seen as good, but goodness that bends for approval doesn't inspire trust — it inspires pity. You can't respect someone who's afraid to disappoint you. And you can't desire someone you don't respect.

The Nice Guy has spent so long trying to avoid rejection that he's lost the very qualities that make him magnetic. Attraction is built on polarity — on contrast, on the spark between strength and softness. But he erases that contrast by trying to be everything she wants. He adapts instead of leading. He agrees instead of asserting. He compliments instead of connecting. And because he's always chasing comfort, he never creates tension — the one thing that makes desire come alive.

What most men don't realize is that *likability* is the lowest form of influence.

Being liked is safe, but safety doesn't inspire devotion. A man who's obsessed with being liked will never be loved deeply, because love requires honesty — and honesty always risks disapproval. The moment you censor your truth to keep the peace, you lose the very edge that commands respect.

The psychology of the Nice Guy runs deeper than behavior; it's rooted in shame. From a young age, many men are taught that their natural instincts — assertiveness, sexuality, ambition — are dangerous. They're told to tone it down, to behave, to be "good boys." So they learn to hide their power instead of mastering it. They trade rawness for politeness, presence for performance. And while the world rewards them for being "safe," their soul begins to resent it. Because no man can feel alive when he's constantly apologizing for his nature.

That's why the Nice Guy always feels drained. He's living in conflict with himself. Every time he swallows his truth to keep someone comfortable, a piece of his authenticity dies. Every time he avoids conflict to be liked, he reinforces his own invisibility. The world reflects back the energy he gives — uncertain, accommodating, easily overlooked.

He doesn't realize that his craving for approval is actually a form of control. He's trying to manipulate how others see him instead of standing firmly in who he is. It's a quieter kind of insecurity — one that wears a smile and calls itself virtue. But underneath that smile is fear. And fear is never attractive.

There's nothing wrong with being kind. Kindness with backbone is power. But kindness without boundaries becomes servitude. Respect doesn't come from niceness; it comes from authenticity — from saying what you mean, meaning what you say, and standing behind it even if it costs you approval.

The moment a man stops chasing agreement, his energy changes. He becomes unpredictable — not in the sense of chaos, but in the sense of freedom. People no longer know exactly how he'll respond, because he's responding truthfully, not tactically. That unpredictability reawakens polarity. It creates tension. It draws people in. Because real presence isn't about being easy to like; it's about being impossible to ignore.

When a man stops performing for acceptance, he stops living in fragments. His posture straightens. His voice deepens. His eyes meet hers without searching for a reaction. He stops apologizing for taking up space. And in that moment, people start reacting differently to him — not because he's louder or meaner, but because he's *whole*.

Women feel the difference immediately. The Nice Guy seeks permission. The grounded man radiates it. The Nice Guy overexplains. The grounded man lets silence speak for him. The Nice Guy chases attention. The grounded man commands it simply by being rooted in himself.

And yet, this transformation doesn't begin with external behavior — it begins internally, with honesty. To stop being the Nice Guy, a man must confront the truth he's been avoiding: that not everyone will like him, that some people will misunderstand him, that rejection is not a verdict — it's clarity. The man who can sit comfortably in that truth becomes untouchable.

Because once you stop needing approval, you can finally act with authenticity. You can tell the truth without flinching. You can express desire without shame. You can draw boundaries without guilt. You stop performing and start leading — and that shift is magnetic. Respect returns. Desire follows. Life starts to feel simple again.

The world will always reward the men who play safe, but it will never *remember* them. It remembers the men who speak their truth and live by it, even when it's inconvenient. The ones who value alignment over applause. That's what gives a man edge — not arrogance, but integrity.

So if the modern Nice Guy wants to become powerful again, he must unlearn the belief that goodness means being agreeable. Real goodness doesn't fold. It stands. It leads with kindness, but never at the expense of truth. Because truth — even when it's uncomfortable — is what separates a man who pleases from a man who commands. And once that truth returns, so does his edge. The politeness fades. The presence sharpens. He stops asking, *"Do they like me?"* and starts asking, *"Am I living honestly?"* That's when the masculine comes back online — steady, grounded, unapologetic. And from that point forward, his relationships begin to shift too. Not because he's learned a new tactic, but because he's remembered an old truth: respect always precedes attraction. Now that we've seen how approval weakens a man, the next step is clear — to rebuild his edge through honesty, direction, and controlled rebellion. Because rebellion isn't chaos. It's clarity in motion.

Rebuilding Honesty and Edge

Every man reaches a point where he has to decide what kind of peace he wants: the peace that comes from avoiding conflict, or the peace that comes from being in alignment with himself. One is fragile — it depends on keeping everyone else comfortable. The other is unshakable — it comes from knowing that even if the world disagrees, you're still standing on truth.

The road back to masculine power begins the moment a man stops performing and starts telling the truth. That truth doesn't have to roar; it just has to be real. Because honesty is not aggression. It's clarity. And clarity is the foundation of confidence.

Politeness, as most men practice it, is often a mask. It's not kindness; it's self-protection. It's the art of saying what you think people want to hear so they don't withdraw approval. But every time you silence your truth to maintain harmony, you chip away at your own integrity. Eventually, you become polite on the outside and resentful on the inside — smiling while something in you quietly dies.

That's what happened to the modern man. He became fluent in diplomacy but forgot the language of authenticity. He learned to smooth every edge until nothing sharp remained. But attraction, respect, leadership — all of them live on the edge. The edge is what defines shape. Without it, there's no contrast, no depth, no tension. The man who tries to be universally liked ends up blending into the background.

Rebuilding your edge starts with brutal self-honesty. Not in the sense of beating yourself down, but of seeing yourself clearly — where you hesitate, where you lie, where you play small. Every lie, no matter how polite, separates you from your own power. Every truth you tell, even a small one, sharpens your presence. Because truth aligns you. It brings your inner world and outer world into sync. And people can feel that alignment before you say a word.

Being genuine is riskier than being polite because honesty doesn't guarantee approval. But that's exactly what makes it powerful. The man who can tell the truth without flinching is signaling something primal — that he doesn't depend on others for safety. He's not reckless; he's free. And that freedom radiates through every part of his being.

You can feel it when he speaks. There's no performance in his tone. His words don't chase agreement. He says what he believes and lets silence do the rest. That kind of man doesn't need to raise his voice. His calmness becomes command. Because people, consciously or not, trust those who are anchored in truth.

Women feel this even more deeply. A woman's instincts are designed to detect incongruence — when a man's words and energy don't match. The polite man who hides behind flattery or careful phrasing may seem nice, but she senses something missing. His energy feels uncertain. But when a man speaks plainly — even imperfectly — she relaxes. She feels his certainty. She may not always agree with him, but she trusts him. And trust is the soil attraction grows from.

Honesty, then, is not just a moral choice. It's a magnetic one. It signals strength, stability, and self-trust — three qualities that define true masculine energy. When you stop lying to protect feelings, you stop living in fear of them. You stop filtering yourself through the expectations of others. You become comfortable with discomfort. And that's the moment your presence deepens.

To rebuild edge, you have to get comfortable being misunderstood. Some people won't like the new version of you — the one who says no, who speaks plainly, who stops apologizing for existing. That's fine. Their discomfort is proof that your boundaries are working. The goal isn't to be harsh; it's to be clear. Clarity may cause friction, but friction creates spark. And that spark is what brings life back to a man's voice, his posture, his energy.

Start small. Say what you mean when it matters. Stop overexplaining. Stop softening every statement with "sorry" or "if that's okay." Speak once, clearly, and let the silence carry the weight of your words. You'll feel awkward at first — like walking without armor. But the more you do it, the more natural it becomes. The fear fades. The tension turns into power. You begin to trust yourself again.

There's a reason why truth feels sharp — it cuts away what's false. And what's false in a man always becomes heavy over time. The lies he tells to keep the peace end up suffocating him. But when he starts living honestly, everything lightens. Decisions become simple. Relationships become cleaner. Life starts to align around authenticity rather than performance.

The edge isn't about arrogance or rebellion for its own sake. It's about wholeness — reclaiming the parts of yourself you muted to stay liked. It's the strength to say, *this is who I am*, and the grace to let others respond however they need to. That's real power — not control over others, but mastery over yourself.

The moment you return to honesty, you also return to polarity. Because polarity isn't about domination — it's about direction. When you stand in truth, people feel drawn to you because you're anchored in something deeper than approval. Your energy becomes grounded, certain, unmoving. In a world full of noise, that steadiness is rare. And rare things are always magnetic. Politeness may open doors, but honesty opens respect.

And once you've rebuilt respect — first with yourself, then with others — confidence follows effortlessly. Because confidence isn't a mood. It's the side effect of integrity. When your words, actions, and values align, you stop performing. You simply exist as you are.

That's the paradox: when you stop trying to be impressive, you become unforgettable. When you stop trying to be liked, you become respected.

And when you stop hiding your truth, you start radiating something that no amount of charm can replicate — authenticity.

That's what brings your edge back. Not louder words or harder stares, but quiet certainty. Not aggression, but alignment. The world bends around the man who no longer bends himself. Because once you've tasted the freedom of living honestly, you'll never go back to pleasing. You'll start to see politeness for what it was like, a cage built from fear. And when that cage falls away, a different kind of rebellion begins — one rooted not in chaos, but in control.

Rebellion Against Weakness

Every era has its rebellion. Once, rebellion meant breaking rules, defying authority, rejecting systems that tried to control the human spirit. But in this age, the real rebellion looks different. It's not loud. It's not chaotic. It doesn't come with smoke or slogans. The modern rebellion is quieter — it lives in the man who refuses to be ruled by his own weakness.

Because weakness, today, doesn't look like failure. It looks like distraction. It looks like comfort disguised as success. It looks like constant reaction — to news, to comments, to cravings, to emotion. The modern man is told he's free, but he's addicted to everything that dulls him: screens, approval, comfort, stimulation. He's not being ruled by dictators anymore. He's being ruled by impulses. That's why discipline has become the new rebellion. Focus has become the new danger. Stillness has become the new strength.

Society doesn't know what to do with a man who moves slowly and deliberately, who chooses restraint over reaction. He can't be manipulated through outrage or dopamine. He doesn't take the bait. While the world is shouting, he's silent. While others chase stimulation, he's sharpening himself in solitude. That kind of man unnerves people — not because he's aggressive, but because he's unshakable.

Rebellion isn't about doing the opposite of what you're told. It's about choosing your path with precision and then walking it without apology. It's not wildness; it's awareness. The man who masters himself doesn't need to perform resistance. His very calmness is defiance. His composure in chaos exposes the hysteria of the world around him.

True rebellion is self-control — the refusal to let your lesser impulses dictate your greater purpose. It's the quiet discipline of doing what must be done, even when no one is watching. It's the choice to stay focused when the world begs for your distraction. To train when no one claps. To walk away when ego wants you to argue.

That's what strength really is: the ability to remain centered while everything around you pulls for reaction. Shouting takes no power; silence does. Anger burns quickly; control burns forever. The loud man seeks dominance to feel strong. The grounded man needs no dominance at all — he leads through gravity. When he enters a room, energy shifts not because he demands it, but because he commands himself.

Weakness hides behind emotion. It hides behind indulgence, excuses, and noise. But when a man rebels against weakness, he learns to sit in discomfort and use it as fuel. Every craving becomes a test. Every challenge becomes a forge. Discipline is not restriction — it's redirection. It takes the energy you've been wasting on distraction and focuses it toward purpose.

That's what separates the ordinary from the exceptional. The ordinary man looks for permission to rest. The exceptional man rests only when he's earned it. The ordinary man waits for motivation. The exceptional man moves from devotion. Because he knows motivation is fleeting, but devotion — to growth, to truth, to mastery — is permanent.

Discipline isn't glamorous. It doesn't post well on social media. It's early mornings, quiet repetition, the subtle power of consistency. It's making the choice that doesn't give you a rush but gives you respect. It's delaying pleasure to earn pride. And the irony is that once you live this way, your energy becomes magnetic. The world starts responding to you differently. Opportunities align. People listen. Women feel the certainty in your energy. Because they can sense that your impulses no longer own you — you own them.

Stillness is the purest form of that ownership. Stillness isn't passivity. It's containment — the ability to hold tension without collapsing. A man who can sit still, breathe deeply, and think clearly under pressure is far more dangerous than one who shouts and swings. The world confuses chaos with strength because it fears calm.

But calm men have always been the most powerful. They don't need to announce their dominance; they embody it.

That's why the strongest men rarely talk about strength. They live it quietly. You see it in their posture, in their eyes, in the deliberate pace of their actions. They're not chasing every impulse, not responding to every emotion. They move when it's time to move. They speak when their words matter. They are disciplined not because they fear losing control, but because they *are* control.

Every man has both forces within him — the weak one that seeks comfort, and the strong one that seeks mastery. One wants ease. The other wants evolution. The weak one begs for validation. The strong one creates it. Rebellion is the choice between those two voices, made every day, in every moment. Every rep in the gym, every hard conversation, every moment of stillness — all of it is an act of defiance against weakness.

And that defiance doesn't harden you. It purifies you. You stop wasting your energy on temporary pleasures and start investing it in permanent power. Your focus sharpens. Your speech slows. Your movements carry weight. You start to look like a man who can handle anything because you can.

That's the quiet revolution — a man who's mastered himself. He doesn't need to project power. He *is* power. He doesn't need to chase rebellion. He *embodies* it.

The world can't sell him distractions because he's already full. It can't control him through fear because he's already faced it. It can't tempt him with noise because he's learned to thrive in silence. That's how you reclaim your masculine edge — not by shouting, but by *stilling*. Not by rebellion in chaos, but by rebellion in control. Because control is the highest form of freedom. And when a man reaches that level of discipline — when he can master his impulses, align his energy, and lead himself with clarity — he stops reacting to the world. He starts directing it. Once you've seen the cage, you can't unsee it. Now it's time to become the man who walks out — not by rage, but by mastery.

From Reaction to Leadership

The first half of a man's life is often spent in reaction. He reacts to expectations — from his parents, from society, from women, from his own insecurities. He reacts to praise by chasing more of it, and to criticism by shrinking smaller. His actions, though constant, aren't truly his. They're responses — reflexes built on fear, validation, and habit. And for a while, he can mistake all that motion for momentum.

But eventually, something breaks. A quiet realization surfaces in the spaces between distractions: *I've been living on everyone else's rhythm but my own.*

That moment marks the beginning of transformation — when reaction starts to feel like a cage, and leadership becomes the only path left that feels true.

Because leadership isn't about controlling others. It's about directing energy — your own first, and everything around you second. It's what happens when you stop letting external forces dictate your internal state. The man who reacts is owned by circumstance. The man who leads shapes it.

The difference lies in awareness. Reaction is impulsive; leadership is intentional. Reaction is emotion-led; leadership is value-led. The man who reacts is constantly chasing balance; the man who leads *is* balance. And that's what gives him presence — not perfection, but poise. He knows what matters, so he moves with clarity. He knows who he is, so he doesn't need to prove it.

This shift from reacting to leading is subtle, but it changes everything. The reactive man speaks quickly, explains too much, and gives his energy away cheaply. The leading man listens first, moves second, and speaks last — not from hesitation, but from choice. He's deliberate because his energy is expensive. He doesn't rush to respond, because he's not seeking approval. He chooses his words the way a craftsman chooses tools — precisely, purposefully, with intent.

That's what women, colleagues, and the world at large feel when they encounter him. It's not charisma in the traditional sense. It's gravity. People trust him not because he's loud, but because he's *consistent*. His emotions don't swing wildly with circumstance. He can feel deeply without being ruled by feeling. His strength comes from containment — the ability to channel chaos instead of becoming it.

Reaction is what the world trains you for. From childhood, you're rewarded for compliance — for doing what's expected, for answering quickly, for adapting instantly. But leadership is the opposite. Leadership requires restraint. It requires stillness in the face of pressure. It asks you to step back, breathe, and decide — not as the world tells you, but as your principles demand.

That's why the path to masculine power isn't about adding more — it's about subtracting noise until what remains is direction. When a man stops reacting, he starts creating. When he stops chasing, he starts choosing. And when he stops seeking permission, he begins to lead.

This shift transforms not only how others see you, but how you see yourself. Your movements gain purpose. Your speech carries authority. Your relationships change — some fall away, others strengthen — because the energy that once leaked out through reaction now fuels presence. You stop needing to prove worthiness, and start expressing it through action.

The reactive man is ruled by emotion. The leading man rules through emotion — not suppressing it, but mastering it. He doesn't run from his anger, desire, or fear; he channels them. Every strong feeling becomes fuel. Every obstacle becomes training. Every challenge becomes a mirror reflecting back who he's choosing to be.

And that's what leadership really is — the conscious choice of direction. It's not about power over others; it's about power over self. The man who can lead himself through chaos, through temptation, through doubt — that man doesn't just survive the modern world. He shapes it.

You can feel it in his stillness. The world pushes, but he doesn't budge. People project onto him, and he stays grounded. He doesn't argue, doesn't prove, doesn't flinch. His focus is precise, his attention measured, his energy sacred. He is no longer playing defense against life — he's moving forward, one intentional step at a time.

That's the transformation you've been building toward throughout this first section — from noise to presence, from performance to authenticity, from reaction to direction. You've stripped away distraction, silence has returned, honesty has been rebuilt, and now discipline has forged structure. What's left is a man who no longer needs to be told who he is.

Because he *knows*.

He's done performing. He's done chasing. He's ready to lead — not from ego, but from alignment. And that's where the next stage begins. Part II is not about rebellion anymore — it's about refinement. It's where we turn principles into power. It's where the man you've been remembering learns to move with precision — to channel his instincts, direct his energy, and master his magnetism. Once you've seen the cage, you can't unsee it. Now it's time to become the man who walks out — not by rage, but by mastery.

The Bad Boy Formula

There's no secret script to becoming magnetic. No trick. No fake confidence. No act. What makes a man stand out — what makes women pay attention without knowing why — is the way he moves through the world. His mindset. His energy. The way he handles pressure. The way he doesn't try too hard but still owns the room. That's what this formula is about.

Not becoming someone else, but reconnecting with the version of you that **already has it** — the edge, the focus, the calm presence that draws people in. The version isn't reaching for approval, because he doesn't need it. This isn't a gimmick. It's a structure — something you can build into how you think, how you show up, and how you lead.

The **Bad Boy Formula** is made up of seven core pieces:

- **F** – Fearless Mindset
- **O** – Own Your Energy
- **R** – Rules of Rebellion
- **M** – Magnetic Habits
- **U** – Unshakable Standards
- **L** – Leadership
- **A** – Attraction

Each one is part of the whole. Together, they reshape how you carry yourself — not just around women, but in every part of your life. You don't need to master all of them at once. But as you move through each one, you'll start to feel it — that shift in how people respond to you, and more importantly, how you respond to yourself. Let's break it down, one piece at a time.

F – Fearless Mindset (Concept)

The Roots of Fear and Validation - Every boy is born wild. Before the world touches him, he moves with instinct. He reaches for what he wants. He explores without hesitation. He doesn't ask if he's allowed — he simply acts, learns, adjusts, and keeps moving. That raw freedom is what gives him life, presence, and power. But somewhere between boyhood and manhood, that wildness gets trained out of him.

He learns the rules — not the ones written in law, but the silent ones. The ones that say, *don't be too loud, don't be too honest, don't want too much, don't make others uncomfortable*. He learns that approval is safer than authenticity, that permission is the path to love, and that validation is the currency of acceptance.

And that's how most men lose their fire — not through defeat, but through domestication.

From a young age, he's rewarded for obedience, not courage. Teachers praise him for following directions. Parents scold him for defiance. He learns that safety lives in compliance, and risk leads to punishment. Every act of rebellion, every surge of boldness, is quietly replaced with hesitation. Over time, that hesitation becomes identity. He stops testing boundaries and starts shrinking inside them.

By the time he becomes an adult, fear has been woven into his sense of self. Not fear of danger, but fear of disapproval. Fear of rejection. Fear of being seen as too much, too confident, too assertive, too masculine. The modern man isn't ruled by external authority — he's ruled by invisible judgment. Every decision, every word, every action runs through the filter: *Will they like this? Will they approve? Will they stay?*

That's the root of validation addiction. It's not just about wanting praise — it's about needing it to feel safe.

Fear and validation are twins. One creates the other. When you depend on approval, fear becomes your compass. You don't move toward what's right; you move toward what's accepted. You don't say what's true; you say what's safe. You don't act with direction; you act with hesitation. And the tragedy is that this fear masquerades as humility. It sounds reasonable — "I just don't want to offend," "I just want to be respectful," "I just don't want to make a mistake."

But beneath those polite sentences is something far more dangerous: submission. Not to another person, but to fear itself.

Because every time you act from fear, you reinforce it. Every time you seek permission, you confirm that you don't believe in your own authority. And every time you trade truth for comfort, you tell your nervous system that safety matters more than sovereignty. Over time, your instincts stop speaking. Your intuition goes quiet. You lose the signal that once guided you.

That's what fear really costs a man — not his opportunities, but his instincts.

The fearless mindset isn't about erasing fear; it's about seeing it clearly and refusing to be ruled by it. Courage isn't the absence of fear — it's the decision that something else matters more. The man who leads himself isn't fearless because he feels nothing. He's fearless because he acts even when the fear is loud. He knows that permission and power can't coexist. You can't wait to be chosen and still claim to lead.

That's the paradox that traps so many men. They want confidence, but they still chase validation. They want respect, but they still ask for it. They want to feel powerful, but they still outsource permission to others — especially to women.

Validation-seeking is subtle. It hides in compliments that secretly crave reciprocation. It hides in texts sent too soon, in jokes told for approval, in silence kept to avoid disagreement. It's the voice that says, *If she approves, I'm worthy*. But that voice is the enemy of masculine freedom. Because the moment you tie your sense of worth to someone else's reaction, you hand them the keys to your self-esteem.

The "bad boy" — the archetype this book reclaims — isn't fearless because he was born that way. He's fearless because he stopped negotiating with fear. He recognized that the only approval that matters is his own. His power doesn't come from rebellion against others; it comes from obedience to his own truth.

That's the difference between boys and men. Boys ask for permission; men give direction. Boys chase reassurance; men create certainty. Boys act from fear of losing love; men act from love of purpose.

And that shift doesn't happen by accident. It happens when you start to question every pattern that fear built in you. When you notice the subtle ways you self-censor. When you recognize that hesitation is not humility — it's control in disguise. Fear pretends to protect you, but what it really does is shrink your life down to what feels comfortable. And comfort kills the masculine spirit.

You can't lead while playing small. You can't create impact while asking for permission. You can't attract powerful energy while radiating uncertainty. Every time you hesitate, you lose presence. Every time you seek approval, you lose polarity. And every time you silence yourself to fit in, you lose the one thing the world needs from you most — your raw, unfiltered direction.

Fearless men aren't born; they're made through confrontation. They look fear in the eye, not to destroy it, but to understand it. They study its patterns — where it hides, how it speaks, what it tries to protect. Then they move anyway. That's how leadership is built — one act of courage at a time.

Because the moment you stop needing to be liked, you start becoming trusted. The moment you stop asking for permission, people start looking to you for direction. Fear loses its grip not when you silence it, but when you outgrow it.

That's the beginning of the *Fearless Mindset* — the foundation of the Bad Boy Formula. It's not recklessness, not arrogance, not defiance for its own sake. It's the reclamation of inner authority — the calm conviction that says, *I decide who I am. I decide what I want. I decide how I move.*

From that state, everything changes. Your words gain weight. Your body language steadies. Your relationships shift. The world starts to respond to your conviction instead of your need.

And that's where courage begins to take form — not as a mood, but as a discipline.

Because the fearless man doesn't chase security; he creates it.

F – Fearless Mindset (Application)

The Quiet Expression of Courage - Real courage doesn't announce itself. It doesn't roar or demand recognition. It moves quietly, like a steady pulse beneath the surface. You can feel it in the way a man breathes, the way he speaks, the way he holds a gaze without flinching. Courage, in its purest form, is not noise — it's composure. It's not rebellion for attention; it's sovereignty in motion.

When a man embodies the fearless mindset, you see it in the spaces between his actions. He doesn't rush to fill silence. He doesn't overexplain. He's not chasing control, because he's already anchored in it. His power lives in the pauses — those small, charged moments where weaker men would crumble under discomfort. Courage isn't what he does when he's certain; it's how he behaves when he's not.

Detachment is where that courage begins. Not emotional numbness, but emotional control — the ability to hold desire, fear, and uncertainty without being ruled by them. The detached man still feels deeply; he simply refuses to be consumed by feeling. He can want without clinging. He can care without chasing. He can love without losing himself.

Detachment is misunderstood because the world equates it with coldness. But detachment is what allows warmth to mean something. A man who's enslaved by emotion burns out quickly; a man who's centered within it radiates steadily. Detachment isn't the absence of care — it's the mastery of it. It's the space that allows composure to exist.

And composure is the most underrated form of strength. In a culture that confuses loudness with leadership, composure is rebellion. When others rush to react, the composed man waits. He observes. He reads the room, the tone, the timing. His restraint unsettles people because it exposes how easily they give their power away. The man who can stay calm under pressure doesn't just survive stress — he commands it.

You can see this difference everywhere — in arguments, negotiations, relationships. The reactive man talks fast, defends himself, and fills the silence with justification. The fearless man lets the silence expand. He doesn't defend his worth because he knows it. He doesn't argue to prove he's right; he acts in alignment and lets reality confirm it over time. That kind of restraint is not passivity — it's precision.

This is what makes the *bad boy* energy so magnetic. It's not the attitude. It's the calibration. He's not detached because he doesn't care — he's detached because he refuses to panic. His composure is contagious. Around him, chaos slows down. People begin to match his rhythm without realizing it. That's what real leadership feels like — not the force of control, but the pull of stability.

Women especially sense this. Their intuition is wired to detect emotional steadiness, to feel whether a man's energy can hold her intensity without collapsing. When she feels that grounded calm — when his presence stays consistent regardless of her emotion — she relaxes. Her guard lowers. She feels safe enough to express, to feel, to trust. It's not logic; it's instinct. A woman can't explain why the composed man draws her in — she just feels it in her nervous system. That's the quiet reward of composure: respect. Respect from men, attraction from women, trust from both.

And it all stems from one thing — truth. Truth is the engine of fearlessness. Detachment and composure are meaningless without it. Because if you're calm but dishonest, you're not powerful — you're performing. Truth gives composure its weight. It's what allows a man to stand still under pressure and know that he doesn't need to hide.

Living in truth requires courage because it exposes you. It means saying what you mean even when it risks connection. It means walking away from what doesn't align, even when it looks comfortable. It means holding your boundaries not because it's easy, but because it's necessary.

Courage shows up in moments that seem small to the outside world but feel enormous inside you. It's when you say no without apology. It's when you tell the truth even though your voice shakes. It's when you stop texting first, not out of manipulation, but because you've stopped chasing validation. It's when you hold eye contact without needing to fill the silence. It's when you stop flinching at your own reflection and start meeting it. That's what the fearless mindset looks like in practice — a thousand quiet decisions to stay aligned when it would be easier to bend. Every act of composure strengthens your authority. Every act of detachment protects your power. Every act of truth reclaims your freedom. The fearless man is not untouched by fear. He simply knows that fear is a signal, not a stop sign. When uncertainty arrives, he doesn't escape it with distraction or noise. He pauses. Breathes. Decides. Then he moves — slowly, deliberately, like a man who knows that leadership doesn't mean avoiding fear but walking through it without losing rhythm.

Fearless men move differently. They speak less, listen more, and act only when necessary. Their courage isn't performative; it's embodied. It's in the stillness of their face, the steadiness of their tone, the patience in their posture. They don't react — they direct. And that's what makes their presence unforgettable. People may not always agree with them, but they can't ignore them. Because truth, when spoken from composure, carries a kind of gravity that can't be faked. It lands. It lingers. It leads.

That's the essence of the fearless mindset — courage as calm, detachment as depth, truth as direction. When a man lives that way, his energy shifts permanently. He stops chasing freedom and starts embodying it. And once you begin to embody it, you realize something powerful: Fear was never the enemy. Fear was the map. It showed you every place you still needed to lead yourself.

O – Own Your Energy (Concept)

Emotional Control and Awareness of Your State - Every man radiates something before he ever opens his mouth. Long before he speaks, the world can already feel him. His presence communicates through subtle channels — his posture, his breathing, the look in his eyes, the pace of his movements. All of these send signals that say far more than words ever could. This is why two men can walk into the same room and be received completely differently. One carries an energy that feels uncertain, scattered, or restless. The other moves with a kind of grounded ease — slow, deliberate, self-contained. People may not consciously understand the difference, but they feel it immediately. That difference is energy. And energy, not language, is what truly speaks first.

Before a man utters a word, his energy has already begun the conversation. It tells others how much he values himself, how centered he is, and how much chaos or clarity lives inside him. Women are especially attuned to this. They read energy faster than logic. A woman doesn't need to hear a man talk to know whether she can trust him, respect him, or relax around him. She can sense it in seconds. This is why mastering your energy matters more than mastering your lines. Because energy precedes words, and people respond not to what you say but to what you transmit.

The problem is that most men were never taught to feel their own energy. They've been raised to think, not to sense. To analyze, not to notice. They live in their heads, constantly strategizing, explaining, and performing, while their bodies quietly store anxiety, tension, and suppressed emotion. They call it "control," but it isn't. Suppression is not strength — it's self-avoidance. The body keeps score of every unacknowledged feeling, and it leaks that energy out in subtle ways: the shaky tone when speaking, the forced laughter in uncomfortable silence, the restless fidgeting during quiet moments. You can't fake calm when your nervous system is screaming chaos.

To own your energy, you must first learn to feel it. Awareness is the gateway to control. Every emotion you experience carries information, not threat. Fear, anger, desire, shame — all of them are signals, not enemies. When you ignore those signals, they start to control you from the shadows. But when you bring awareness to them, you regain the power to choose your response. Emotional control doesn't mean suppressing what you feel. It means observing it without letting it decide who you'll be in that moment. It's the difference between having emotions and being possessed by them. The man who can feel anger without collapsing into aggression, or feel fear without fleeing from it, becomes powerful not because he avoids emotion, but because he directs it.

Emotional regulation is the quiet foundation of masculinity. It's what allows composure under pressure and confidence in uncertainty. True control is not about keeping a straight face while your heart races; it's about mastering your inner state so deeply that your environment no longer dictates it. You can be standing in chaos and still feel centered. You can be provoked and still remain calm. You can be tempted and still choose clarity. This doesn't make you cold — it makes you steady. And steadiness is what creates presence. When the world realizes it cannot easily shake you, it begins to respect you.

Women sense this instantly. They can feel when a man's energy is grounded and when it's scattered. They know when his attention is whole and when it's divided. They feel when his composure is real and when it's a mask. The feminine, by nature, is movement — emotional, expressive, fluid. It flows like water and thrives when it meets a strong container. The masculine provides that container not through dominance, but through emotional mastery. The grounded man doesn't silence her expression; he stabilizes it. He doesn't control her; he controls himself, and that's what allows her to feel safe in his presence. Safety doesn't mean dullness — it means she can open fully without fearing collapse. His stillness gives her permission to be free.

Owning your energy means developing that kind of awareness every single day. It means noticing how your mood shifts when you wake up, how your breath shortens under stress, how your body reacts to certain people or environments. It means becoming fluent in your own state so that you're no longer surprised by your emotions. When you know yourself that well, you stop reacting to life and start directing it. The man who can name what he's feeling can also decide what he'll do with it. That's power — not external, but internal. The man who commands his own energy commands the energy of any room he walks into.

Energy control also means conservation. Every time you overexplain yourself, argue online, chase attention, or indulge in negativity, you spend your energy recklessly. You hand your power over to anything that can provoke a reaction. Owning your energy is learning to protect it. It's choosing where your attention goes, because attention is your life force. When you stop scattering it across meaningless noise, you start to feel stronger, more centered, more alive. Your calm becomes heavier, your silence more eloquent. You stop trying to prove and start allowing. That's when confidence begins to feel effortless.

Confidence, at its core, is energetic consistency. It's the alignment between how you feel and how you show up. When your inner state is calm and your outer presence matches it, people can feel the integrity. That's why certain men can say very little yet hold an entire room — their energy is coherent. There are no mixed signals, no hidden insecurity disguised as charm. Their presence says everything their words don't need to. The more consistent your energy, the more magnetic your life becomes. Opportunities appear, relationships deepen, and people start responding not to what you demand, but to what you *emanate*.

To own your energy is to become a thermostat rather than a thermometer. Most men reflect the temperature of their environment — they're cheerful when things go well, frustrated when they don't. Their moods rise and fall with circumstance. A thermostat, on the other hand, sets the temperature. When you walk into a room grounded, composed, and aware, you shift the energy around you. People subconsciously adjust to your pace, your rhythm, your stillness. That is leadership at the most primal level — not through words, but through vibration.

Ultimately, mastering energy is mastering presence. It's the discipline of returning to center no matter what happens outside you. It's walking through the world with the awareness that your internal state dictates your external reality. You can't fake it, and you can't outsource it. The only way to embody it is through practice — through daily awareness, through breath, through silence, through restraint. When you live this way, your emotions become allies instead of enemies. Your energy becomes a force that builds rather than drains.

And the more you align with that steady inner rhythm, the more people feel it without knowing why. Women lean closer. Men listen longer. Opportunities open. Not because you've said the right thing, but because your energy says, *I'm unshakable*. It's an unspoken language — one the world always understands.

That is the essence of owning your energy: emotional control rooted in awareness, composure that doesn't come from suppression but from clarity, and the understanding that everything you project begins inside you. When you master your state, your words gain weight, your silence becomes presence, and your life starts to move in rhythm with your power. Because in the end, it's not your voice that leads — it's your energy.

O – Own Your Energy (Application)

The Art of Embodied Presence - Presence isn't an act. It's not a look you put on or a line you rehearse. It's the state of being completely rooted in yourself — fully here, fully alive, fully unbothered. Every movement, every breath, every silence you hold communicates something long before your words ever do. You've probably felt this before: someone walks into a room, says nothing, yet everyone notices. Not because they demand attention, but because they *embody* it. That's not charisma. That's coherence — their mind, body, and energy are all aligned in the same direction.

To live in that kind of presence, you must first learn to slow down. The modern man moves too quickly. He rushes his speech, his gestures, his thoughts. Speed is often a symptom of anxiety — a way of escaping the discomfort of stillness. But the slower a man moves, the more deliberate he becomes. He walks into a space and takes a moment before he speaks. He doesn't rush to fill silence or prove his value. He lets the world come to him instead of chasing it. That pacing alone changes everything. You stop leaking uncertainty, and your calm begins to create gravity.

Your body language is the first language people read. Before you ever speak, you're telling the world how to treat you. The way you stand, the way you breathe, the way you occupy space — all of it reveals your relationship with yourself. The man who collapses his posture signals doubt. The man who fidgets signals insecurity. The man who tries too hard to appear relaxed signals performance. But the man who stands tall, shoulders open, spine straight, and breath slow doesn't need to signal anything — his body speaks clarity. There's no pretense in his stance. It's natural authority — the kind that makes people instinctively pay attention.

Your breath is the anchor of that authority. Shallow breathing is the language of anxiety. When you breathe from your chest, your body stays in fight-or-flight. You talk faster, think faster, and feel easily shaken. Deep, controlled breathing — from the diaphragm, slow and steady — changes everything. It tells your nervous system that you're safe. It grounds your thoughts and regulates your emotions. And when your breath slows, your voice follows. Your tone deepens, your words stretch, and your entire presence feels heavier — not forced, but firm. The man who breathes deeply moves like someone who doesn't need to hurry, because his time belongs to him.

Tone is the next level of presence. You can say the exact same words in two different states and get two entirely different reactions. A rushed tone projects insecurity; a steady tone commands attention. When you speak slowly, without urgency, it signals self-trust. You're not trying to convince anyone. You're sharing what you already know. A grounded tone doesn't shout or strain. It flows from the chest, not the throat. It carries confidence, not volume. Women, in particular, respond to this unconsciously. A man's tone tells her more about his presence than his words ever will. She doesn't just hear what he's saying — she *feels* whether he's centered while saying it.

Eye contact is another language of energy. Most men either avoid it or overuse it. Avoidance communicates timidity; staring communicates control issues. True presence is somewhere between — steady, calm, unhurried. It's not about locking eyes to dominate; it's about holding them with ease. When you can maintain eye contact without flinching, without needing a reaction, without filling the silence, you project calm authority. Your gaze says, *I'm here. I see you. I don't need anything from you.* That combination of attention and detachment is magnetic.

Women feel these cues on a biological level. Before they consciously process your words, their nervous system is reading your energy — scanning for steadiness, safety, congruence. She feels whether your body and your words match. If your posture is confident but your eyes dart around, her instincts will sense the mismatch and withdraw. If your voice is deep but forced, she'll feel the tension behind it. But if your tone, breath, and gaze are aligned — relaxed but certain — she doesn't need logic to feel drawn in. Her body relaxes before her mind understands why. That's the silent communication of presence: safety that excites, calm that attracts.

You don't need to perform this. Presence isn't about doing more — it's about removing what's unnecessary. You don't have to fake calmness or confidence; you only need to stop interrupting them. When your body is relaxed, your breath slow, and your mind quiet, you return to your natural masculine rhythm. Everything else follows. Conversations flow. Tension builds in a way that feels alive, not anxious. You stop chasing connection and start creating it just by existing fully in the moment.

This is what women respond to, even if they can't articulate it. They're not reacting to your looks or your words — they're reacting to your *state*. When your energy is grounded, they feel safe enough to express their feminine energy fully. The polarity between stillness and movement, structure and flow, calm and expression — that's what creates chemistry. It's not manipulation. It's resonance. When your body is calm, her body relaxes. When your breath is steady, hers deepens. When your voice is grounded, her guard lowers. Presence is contagious.

Practicing presence doesn't require elaborate techniques. It starts with awareness — noticing your state before you walk into any room, before you text, before you speak. Take one deep breath before you respond. Feel your feet on the ground. Relax your shoulders. Let silence live between your words. This is how presence becomes muscle memory — not through force, but through repetition. Over time, your energy settles into a rhythm that others can trust.

Owning your energy at this level makes your life simpler. You stop needing to chase validation or control outcomes. You realize that influence isn't about doing more — it's about *being more*. The more you embody calm certainty, the less you need to prove anything. People sense it. Women lean in. The world adjusts. It's not magic. It's physics — the world always orbits around what's stable.

Presence is the final expression of self-mastery. It's your inner stillness made visible, your alignment turned physical. When your breath, tone, and body language all move in the same rhythm, you become impossible to ignore — not because you're demanding attention, but because you've stopped leaking it. You're no longer chasing the moment; you *are* the moment.

That's what it means to own your energy — to move through life as a man whose silence speaks louder than other men's words, whose stillness commands more attention than another's noise, and whose presence changes the room without effort. Once you reach that point, you stop trying to be noticed. You simply are. And that's where true magnetism begins.

R – Rules of Rebellion (Concept)

Integrity as the New Revolution - Rebellion used to mean noise. It meant breaking rules, burning bridges, and defying everything that came before. The rebel was loud, unpredictable, and reckless — a man who proved his strength by destroying what others built. But the deeper truth is that real rebellion isn't chaos. Real rebellion is control. It's the art of knowing when to move, when to resist, and when to walk away. It's the discipline of saying "no" when every weak instinct in you wants to say "yes."

To understand true rebellion, you have to look at what the world wants from you. The modern world doesn't ask you to conform by force; it seduces you with comfort. It wants you agreeable, available, and endlessly entertained. It rewards obedience not through punishment, but through convenience. It tells you to scroll instead of think, to please instead of lead, to chase instead of choose. And every time you comply, your edge dulls a little more. You become another man reacting instead of directing — another man who mistakes noise for purpose.

That's why rebellion now looks different. It's no longer about raising your fist; it's about mastering your focus. It's about standing in a culture of distraction and choosing clarity. It's about saying "no" to the thousand small temptations that promise pleasure but deliver weakness. Every boundary you draw, every discipline you keep, every standard you hold — that's rebellion. Because the system thrives on your submission, not your strength.

Integrity, then, is the highest form of rebellion. It's what happens when you stop living by reactions and start living by principles. Integrity is not about being perfect or moralistic; it's about being whole. It's the alignment between what you say and what you do, between your inner code and your external actions. And in a world built on image and performance, that kind of consistency is radical. When you live with integrity, you no longer need to shout your values — they show up in your behavior. People feel it. They sense that your "no" means no and your "yes" means yes. You stop negotiating with your boundaries. You stop apologizing for your standards. You stop explaining your decisions to those who don't deserve to influence them.

Saying "no" is one of the hardest things a man can do, not because the word itself is difficult, but because it carries consequences. Saying no means risking disapproval, rejection, and misunderstanding. But that's the point — rebellion always carries a price. Every time you say no to something that weakens you, you say yes to your own strength. Every time you hold a boundary, you fortify your identity. Every time you refuse to be manipulated by guilt or fear, you reclaim your authority.

Rebellion, in this new sense, is quiet. It's not the noise of defiance but the stillness of clarity. The man who lives this way doesn't seek conflict, but he's not afraid of it either. His peace is not the absence of confrontation; it's the presence of conviction. You can't provoke him into reaction because he's not driven by ego. His rebellion isn't against others — it's against the weakness within himself. He rebels against his own laziness, his own impulses, his own need for validation. He's not fighting society; he's mastering his nature.

This kind of rebellion builds power from the inside out. When a man learns to say no to distractions, he starts to focus. When he says no to convenience, he finds discipline. When he says no to validation, he rediscovers self-respect. And when he lives with self-respect, people instinctively trust his leadership. Integrity becomes magnetic. It's rare, and anything rare in this world draws attention.

The ability to say no also redefines relationships. Most men lose power not because they're unkind, but because they can't refuse. They say yes to keep peace, to avoid discomfort, to maintain affection. But that kind of peace is fake — it's purchased with self-betrayal. Real peace comes when your boundaries are clear enough that your soul doesn't have to argue with your mouth. A man who can say no without guilt is a man who's free. He doesn't manipulate, and he doesn't get manipulated. His relationships are built on respect, not compliance. Women feel this instinctively. They might test his boundaries, but they secretly admire the man who holds them. Because boundaries signal direction, and direction signals safety.

This is what separates the grounded man from the "bad boy" stereotype. The reckless rebel says no to everything — rules, structure, discipline — and ends up lost in chaos. The grounded man says no *strategically*. He doesn't reject structure; he defines it. He doesn't fight the system just to fight — he creates his own. His rebellion is selective, surgical, precise. He knows what deserves his energy and what doesn't, and that clarity makes him untouchable.

Integrity-based rebellion also demands solitude. You can't develop a strong "no" if you've never learned to be alone. Weak men fear isolation because they draw their identity from approval. Strong men crave solitude because that's where clarity is born. When you spend time alone — in silence, in stillness — you begin to hear your own voice again. You remember what you stand for. And once you reconnect with that internal compass, no crowd, no woman, no system can pull you off center.

Rebellion is not the refusal of rules; it's the refusal of *misalignment*. You still have a code — in fact, your code becomes everything. It dictates how you work, how you love, how you lead. It tells you what's worth your fight and what isn't. And when you live by that code consistently, life becomes simpler. Choices become cleaner. You stop wasting time on things that drain your energy. You move through the world lighter, sharper, more precise.

To say "no" when it matters is not an act of arrogance — it's an act of integrity. It's how a man declares to himself, *My energy, my time, my peace are sacred.* And every time he honors that declaration, his power grows quietly. He doesn't need rebellion as performance anymore. His boundaries *are* rebellion. His discipline *is* rebellion. His focus *is* rebellion. Because in a world where almost every man is distracted, compliant, and exhausted, the one who lives by self-respect stands out like a flame in fog.

Rebellion, then, is not the opposite of order — it's the creation of a higher one. It's the man who no longer fights the world but shapes it by mastering himself. It's the man whose strength is so steady that even when he says nothing, everyone can feel where he stands.

And that's where true authority begins — in the quiet conviction of a man who no longer needs to explain his boundaries, because he *embodies* them.

R – Rules of Rebellion (Application)

The Magnetic Power of Independence and Unpredictability - The most magnetic men in the world aren't trying to be mysterious. They simply are. Their unpredictability doesn't come from manipulation — it comes from freedom. You never quite know what they'll do next, not because they're playing games, but because they don't live by anyone else's script. That's what draws people in. In a world where everyone moves in predictable loops — scrolling the same feeds, saying the same things, chasing the same outcomes — the man who acts from his own rhythm feels alive. His independence doesn't isolate him; it electrifies him. You can feel it when he walks into a room. He's not scanning faces for approval or gauging what version of himself will be accepted. He's simply present, moving according to his own gravity. He's polite, but not performative. He's warm, but not eager. He's engaged, but not available to everyone. That balance between openness and restraint — between accessibility and mystery — creates tension. And tension is the pulse of attraction.

Unpredictability doesn't mean chaos. It's not about playing hard to get or acting indifferent. True unpredictability comes from independence — from a man whose decisions come from internal clarity, not external validation. When he texts, it's because he means it, not because he's following a rule. When he says no, it's not a test; it's truth. His actions are not reactions to others but expressions of himself. And that kind of self-directed energy is magnetic because it's rare.

People — especially women — are drawn to men who have a life that moves on its own momentum. When a man's world doesn't orbit around anyone else, it creates gravity. You can feel it in subtle ways. He doesn't rush to reply, not out of arrogance, but because his attention is already occupied by something meaningful. He doesn't cancel plans impulsively, because his time has structure. He doesn't explain his decisions endlessly, because they're rooted in purpose, not impulse. Every move he makes feels intentional, and that intention carries weight. That's the paradox of rebellion — the more disciplined you are internally, the more unpredictable you appear externally. Because most men live in patterns of reaction, anyone who operates from genuine self-direction becomes impossible to predict. You can't anticipate a man who's not driven by fear or approval. He's spontaneous not because he's impulsive, but because he's free.

Independence is the quiet center of this magnetism. It's not about isolation; it's about sovereignty. It's the understanding that your energy, attention, and purpose are your own to direct. When you live that way, your relationships change instantly. You stop chasing, stop convincing, stop performing. You start inviting. You create space for others to step into your world instead of trying to squeeze into theirs. That's the masculine dynamic at its purest — not pursuit out of need, but attraction out of wholeness.

When a man is independent, women feel it before they see it. His energy says, *I want you, but I don't need you.* That balance — desire without dependency — is intoxicating. It tells her that his world is full with or without her, and that if she chooses to enter it, it will be by her own will, not his desperation. That's the kind of man a woman can respect, trust, and surrender to — not because he controls her, but because he doesn't need to. His independence gives her the freedom to feel her emotions fully without having to carry his.

Unpredictability, in this sense, becomes a natural byproduct of authenticity. When you no longer operate from fear, you become hard to categorize. You stop following predictable emotional patterns. You might laugh when others expect anger, stay calm when others expect chaos, walk away when others expect a fight. You confuse small minds because you're no longer reacting from ego. You respond from truth. And truth, being alive and evolving, is never entirely predictable.

This is what separates the grounded man from the performer. The performer calculates his moves to appear interesting. The grounded man simply *is* interesting because he's not performing. He's spontaneous within structure, wild within purpose. His life has rhythm, but not routine. He can change plans at a moment's notice without losing direction. He's flexible without being aimless, spontaneous without being reckless. That balance between stability and freedom is what makes him impossible to forget.

The rebel's magnetism also lies in contrast. He can be silent one moment and sharp the next. Calm most days, but unpredictable when the moment calls for it. He moves like a storm that you didn't see coming — not destructive, but undeniable. This contrast keeps people on edge in the best way. It makes women feel both safe and curious. They never fully have him figured out, and that mystery keeps desire alive. But again — it's not an act. It's the natural outcome of living in alignment with yourself.

Independence also shapes how you handle connection. The dependent man fears losing interest; the independent man knows he can create it endlessly. He doesn't cling when distance appears; he lets space do the work. He doesn't demand attention; he earns it through the way he moves. His life — his routines, his mission, his habits — all communicate something beyond words: *I am fulfilled on my own, but I welcome those who add to my fire.* That's why women lean toward him. He's not chasing warmth; he *is* warmth.

Owning your independence doesn't mean rejecting closeness. It means knowing that closeness isn't supposed to consume you. When you stop merging your identity with others, you become whole again. That wholeness is what people crave, even if they can't articulate it. The man who lives for himself — not selfishly, but with direction — gives everyone around him permission to do the same. He becomes a mirror that reminds others of their own power.

And when a man reaches that level of self-possession, unpredictability becomes inevitable. Because you can't predict someone who isn't seeking approval. You can't control someone who doesn't fear loss. You can't manipulate someone who doesn't need your validation. He's free — and freedom, in any form, is magnetic.

This is what rebellion looks like in practice — not destruction, but distinction. The courage to live by your own design, to hold your standards without apology, to let curiosity replace control. You don't rebel by shouting; you rebel by existing on your own terms. You don't perform mystery; you become it by being fully yourself in a world of copies.

The modern rebel doesn't rage against the system. He outgrows it. His power doesn't come from resistance — it comes from refinement. His unpredictability isn't noise — it's the quiet pulse of freedom that makes the world turn to look.

That's how independence becomes magnetism. ot through chaos, but through calm control. Not through mystery, but through mastery.

Because in the end, rebellion isn't about being untamed — it's about being *unowned*.

M – Magnetic Habits (Concept)

Routine as Sacred Ritual - A man's life is built in the moments no one sees. Not in the grand gestures or dramatic choices, but in the quiet repetitions that shape his days. Every habit — the way he wakes, the way he breathes, the way he eats, trains, speaks, and thinks — writes the invisible script of his energy. Over time, those patterns become his aura. You can sense it when you meet him. Some men carry chaos in their rhythm — rushing, scrolling, reacting, running from silence. Others move with calm inevitability, their lives organized around a private code. They are not rigid, but rhythmic. Not mechanical, but intentional. They've turned routine into ritual — and that's what makes their energy magnetic.

Habit is misunderstood in the modern world. People see it as boring, restrictive, a cage that limits spontaneity. But discipline, in its highest form, doesn't limit freedom — it amplifies it. Because every man is ruled by something. If he doesn't choose his structure, chaos chooses it for him. When you live without rhythm, you live at the mercy of impulse. Your energy becomes scattered, your focus diluted, your presence thin. You can't build power without repetition. You can't build presence without rhythm. Magnetism, like mastery, is born from devotion.

Daily habits are how you communicate with your future self. They're quiet promises you keep every day without applause or recognition. The workout you don't skip. The book you finish instead of scrolling. The early morning silence you protect before the world wakes up. Each act seems small, almost insignificant, but together they form the architecture of your identity. Because consistency creates gravity. When your actions align day after day, your energy deepens. You stop floating through life and start moving through it with weight.

That's why routine, when lived consciously, becomes sacred. It's not about control — it's about communion. Every morning routine, every breath practice, every repetition in the gym becomes a dialogue between who you are and who you're becoming. You're teaching your mind that you can be trusted. You're reminding your body that discipline is love, not punishment. Over time, this dialogue creates a quiet confidence that no one can fake. You stop needing motivation because your habits have already made your decisions for you. Discipline becomes identity, and identity becomes energy.

Women sense this instantly. They feel it not in what you say, but in how you move. The man who lives in ritual carries a calm authority that cannot be manufactured. He's not seeking direction from others; he's already found it within himself. His life has order, rhythm, and consistency — qualities that create safety at the energetic level. The feminine instinctively trusts a man whose habits show he can lead himself. She doesn't need to see his bank account or his résumé; she feels his structure in the way he stands, the way he breathes, the way he listens. That trust isn't logical — it's instinctive.

Magnetism grows in men who respect time. When you treat your hours like currency, life starts to treat you like a man of value. Wasted time drains masculine energy faster than anything else. Every aimless hour spent in distraction erodes the sharpness of your presence. But when your days are guided by deliberate rhythm — training your body, sharpening your mind, grounding your emotions — your energy thickens. You start to carry an invisible weight that others can feel. You become a man who seems to "have it together," not because life is easy, but because your foundation is built from daily precision.

Routine also builds spiritual strength. When your actions become consistent, your emotions stop ruling you. You stop waiting for perfect conditions to act. You stop needing to feel ready. The gym becomes a temple, not because of the weights, but because of what those repetitions symbolize — devotion, presence, self-respect. Your morning silence becomes prayer. Your work becomes offering. You begin to live each day like a ritual of alignment. That's the transformation discipline brings: it turns the mundane into meaningful.

There's a reason why ancient warriors, monks, and masters across cultures all lived by ritual. They understood that repetition is not the enemy of passion — it's the forge of it. The more structured your routine, the freer your mind becomes. Because when your body knows what to do, your energy is liberated for creation, direction, and presence. That's why magnetic men always appear calm — their structure carries them. They don't scramble to find purpose each day; their habits already hold it.

Over time, your habits become your aura. They define how you show up, how you breathe, how you hold space. You can tell when a man lives in alignment — his body moves efficiently, his speech has weight, his gaze is steady. That's not luck or personality; it's the reflection of discipline made visible. You can fake charm for an hour, but you can't fake consistency over time. The energy you carry is simply the echo of how you live when no one's watching.

If you want to become magnetic, build a life that charges you daily. Craft habits that sharpen your edges and quiet your mind. Protect your mornings. Train your body. Guard your attention like a sacred resource. Create time for stillness and silence. These aren't chores — they're rituals that remind your system who you are. When your daily rhythm aligns with your deeper purpose, your presence begins to radiate coherence. And coherence — that invisible harmony between action and intention — is what makes a man unforgettable.

Magnetism isn't something you perform; it's something you cultivate. You can't fake the energy of a man who keeps his word to himself. It lives in his walk, his tone, his patience. It's the energy of a man who doesn't need to chase, because he's already found what he's looking for — direction. That direction gives his life rhythm, and that rhythm gives his energy power.

Routine is not a prison. It's a frame. It's what keeps your freedom from turning into chaos. Without structure, passion burns out. With structure, passion becomes art. That's what your habits are — small acts of art that build your future. And when you start to see them that way, even the simplest action — a morning stretch, a journal entry, a disciplined meal — becomes sacred. Because through them, you're not just managing time. You're shaping presence.

In a distracted world, a man of ritual stands out. His energy moves differently — slower, steadier, deliberate. He doesn't need to be the loudest, because consistency amplifies him more than volume ever could. Every choice he repeats is a quiet declaration: *I'm in command of myself.* And that command radiates through everything he touches.

Magnetism is born from rhythm. Rhythm is born from devotion. And devotion, lived daily, is the most powerful rebellion of all.

M – Magnetic Habits (Application)

Lifestyle, Discipline, and Aesthetic Energy - Magnetism is not something you switch on when you leave the house. It's something you build, cell by cell, in the quiet repetitions of your daily life. The man who appears effortlessly attractive isn't lucky; he's aligned. His outer presence is simply a mirror of his inner order. You can't fake that kind of energy because it isn't decoration — it's discipline made visible. The way he moves, dresses, speaks, and breathes all point to the same truth: *this man lives deliberately.* And that deliberate energy is what draws people in.

A magnetic lifestyle is not about perfection — it's about coherence. Every part of your life should communicate the same frequency: direction, awareness, calm control. The clothes you wear, the way you sit, the smell of your home, the music that fills your space — all of it sends a message about who you are. Most men never consider that their environment is constantly shaping their energy. Cluttered space, chaotic habits, lazy posture — they all bleed into the way you move through the world. When you refine your surroundings, you refine your presence. Simplicity becomes a form of power. The fewer distractions you keep, the more your focus sharpens. And when your external world reflects your internal order, people can feel it before they understand it.

Discipline is the engine behind that refinement. It's not punishment — it's preparation. Every disciplined act reinforces your self-trust. When you wake up early, train your body, follow through on commitments, or finish what you start, you're not just building strength — you're building *stability.* The world can feel that stability. Women, especially, sense it instantly. It's in the way you carry yourself: shoulders open, chin steady, steps measured. There's no rush in your energy, no searching in your eyes. A disciplined man doesn't move like he's chasing time; he moves like he owns it. That subtle control — the calm rhythm between action and rest — is deeply attractive because it signals emotional security. It says, *I lead myself.*

Aesthetic magnetism grows naturally from that foundation. The way you present yourself is an extension of your discipline, not vanity. It's not about brands or trends; it's about precision. A man's aesthetic should reflect his essence — clean, intentional, without excess. Well-fitted clothes, well-kept grooming, subtle scent, steady eye contact — these things are not superficial. They're signals of self-respect. When a man takes care of himself, he communicates that he values his energy and expects the same in return. A woman feels that respect before she ever hears his words. She notices how his shirt fits, how his voice carries, how he seems *put together* — not because he's performing, but because he's ordered.

This is how lifestyle becomes language. Every choice you make — from your morning routine to the way you close your day — broadcasts something about your consciousness. A man who lives in chaos radiates chaos. A man who lives in rhythm radiates control. When you integrate discipline into your lifestyle, your energy becomes consistent, and consistency is magnetic. The more consistent you are, the safer people feel in your presence. They don't have to guess which version of you will show up. They know. That predictability in character — combined with unpredictability in expression — creates the perfect balance of safety and mystery.

Women don't fall for your achievements; they fall for your rhythm. They're drawn to how you inhabit your space, how you move through time, how your focus doesn't fracture under distraction. When she speaks, you're not scrolling. When she enters a room, you meet her eyes with calm awareness, not hunger. She feels your attention like warmth — not desperate, but directed. That's the energy of a man who's mastered his habits. His presence isn't scattered; it's singular. He's not waiting for the world to inspire him — he's already generating his own current.

The secret is that magnetism doesn't require effort once your foundation is aligned. Your energy carries the residue of your discipline. The man who trains regularly stands differently. The man who eats with awareness has a different glow. The man who reads daily speaks differently. The man who spends time in silence listens differently. All of these choices, stacked together, create an aura that no cologne or pickup line can replicate. It's not about being perfect; it's about being practiced. The daily rituals polish your rough edges until you move through life with quiet sharpness.

A magnetic lifestyle also balances edge with ease. The disciplined man isn't rigid; he's relaxed. He can laugh easily, adapt smoothly, and shift gears when needed. His confidence doesn't come from control, but from competence. Because when you live by structure, you trust yourself to handle spontaneity. That trust allows you to relax, and that relaxation makes your presence even more potent. Women can feel that too — a man who's serious about his life, but not uptight about it. Purposeful, but playful. Grounded, but alive. That balance between direction and freedom is irresistible.

Your life becomes magnetic the moment it stops looking like a performance and starts feeling like a pulse. When your habits align with your values, your energy begins to hum at a steady frequency — calm, focused, alive. You no longer need to chase momentum; you create it. You no longer need to prove worth; you embody it. And that embodiment changes how people experience you. They start to feel steadier around you, more open, more trusting. That's not manipulation — it's resonance. When your energy is ordered, you create order around you.

Magnetism, then, is not about doing more. It's about living with precision. It's the quiet confidence that comes from knowing your days have meaning, your body has rhythm, and your environment reflects intention. Every habit you build is a declaration of respect for yourself. And that self-respect — lived daily, expressed effortlessly — becomes the energy others feel the moment you walk into a room.

Because in the end, attraction isn't created in the moment you meet someone. It's created in the moments when no one's watching — in the mornings you stay disciplined, in the workouts you finish, in the silence you keep, in the order you maintain. All those invisible acts compound into an energy that moves through you naturally. That's the secret of the magnetic man: he doesn't chase. He simply lives in alignment so powerfully that everything else gravitates toward him.

When your lifestyle, discipline, and aesthetics align, you stop trying to be impressive — you become inevitable.

U – Unshakable Standards (Concept)

How Self-Worth Sets the Tone for Every Interaction - Every man lives according to a standard — the question is whether he chose it consciously or inherited it from the world around him. Most men don't realize that their standards are not declared through words but through tolerance. What you allow, what you chase, what you settle for — that's your real standard. And your life will always rise or fall to match it.

Self-worth is not confidence. Confidence can be faked, performed, borrowed for a night and lost by morning. Self-worth is quieter, deeper, unshakable. It's the internal measurement of value that decides how you move through the world. A man with high self-worth doesn't need to prove his value; he assumes it. That assumption shapes his tone, his boundaries, his choices. It dictates what kind of energy he entertains and what kind he rejects. It decides which opportunities he pursues and which temptations he lets pass. Self-worth is the governor of presence — it controls the quality of everything you attract.

When a man doesn't know his worth, he becomes reactive. He overexplains himself, apologizes unnecessarily, negotiates for validation. His energy feels unstable because it depends on others to define it. The world senses this immediately. People treat him based on the price tag he puts on himself. When you act like your time is cheap, others spend it freely. When you act like your attention is disposable, others take it without gratitude. But when your self-worth is solid — when your silence carries the same authority as another man's shouting — everything shifts. You stop trying to earn respect and start commanding it.

High standards begin with one truth: you are the gatekeeper of your energy. Every time you lower your standards to keep someone close, you tell yourself that your worth is negotiable. And once you teach yourself that, it bleeds into every part of your life. You tolerate mediocrity from friends, disrespect from partners, laziness from yourself. Each small compromise chips away at your confidence until you forget what your power felt like. Rebuilding it starts by remembering this: what you allow is what continues.

Having unshakable standards doesn't mean being harsh or unapproachable. It means being clear. It means knowing what you value and refusing to pretend otherwise. The man with standards doesn't need to raise his voice to draw a line — his boundaries are already written in the way he lives. He doesn't entertain chaos because his peace is expensive. He doesn't chase people because his attention is rare. He doesn't need to prove dominance; his composure does it for him. That's the paradox of true strength: the higher your standards, the calmer you become. Because you're no longer in the business of convincing anyone to respect what you've already decided to protect.

Women feel this instantly. A man with standards doesn't need to announce them — his behavior reveals them. He texts less but with intention. He listens without losing himself in her stories. He's affectionate, but not available to inconsistency. His value isn't determined by her interest, and that independence creates the spark of polarity. She senses his self-respect, and it makes her respect him in return. The dynamic shifts — she doesn't see him as another man trying to earn her approval; she sees him as a man living by a code. And codes are irresistible because they create safety.

Your standards are also your filters. They determine who and what gets access to your inner world. Without them, your energy becomes diluted. You let too many voices in, too many influences, too many distractions. But when you know your worth, your boundaries sharpen naturally. You stop engaging in low-value conversations. You stop wasting time convincing people who don't want to understand. You stop giving your energy to things that don't give energy back. You start living in alignment with your values instead of drifting through other people's expectations.

That alignment creates a kind of authority that can't be imitated. It's the authority of a man who doesn't flinch in silence, who doesn't compromise under pressure, who doesn't chase attention because he already carries his own. It's not arrogance — it's integrity. The world mistakes calm certainty for ego because it's so rare to see. But once you taste it, you'll never go back to performing for approval. Because you'll realize that every "no" rooted in self-worth feels more powerful than a hundred "yeses" born of fear.

Standards are not about being perfect — they're about being consistent. They're the invisible framework that holds your life together when motivation fades. When you keep your word, follow through on your habits, and refuse to compromise your principles, your energy gains density. You become less reactive, more grounded, more magnetic. The man who can say "this is what I tolerate" and live it — even when it costs him — carries a presence that others can't ignore. His energy says: *I am not for everyone, and that's the point.*

High self-worth is contagious. When you live by it, people start adjusting to your frequency. The world respects what you respect. If you treat your time, attention, and body as sacred, others will too. That's why your standards are never just about you — they teach everyone around you how to behave. When you set the tone, you become the conductor of your reality. You decide who gets to play in your symphony and who doesn't.

The truth is, standards aren't boundaries you set for others; they're commitments you make to yourself. They're how you prove your love for your own potential. Because the man who keeps raising his standards is the man who keeps expanding. His relationships evolve. His circle tightens. His confidence deepens. And that's the natural evolution of masculine energy — refinement through clarity.

Unshakable standards transform every interaction because they communicate your worth without you needing to. You can tell when a man lives by them — his energy doesn't sway with compliments or criticism. Praise doesn't inflate him, and rejection doesn't break him. He remains steady because his value was never on the line. That steadiness is the real definition of power. Not control over others, but control over self.

A man's standards are his gravity. They define how deeply he moves, how clearly he sees, and how strongly he pulls the world around him into order. The higher the standard, the calmer the energy. The calmer the energy, the louder the presence. That's the formula. Because in a culture that rewards compromise and calls it kindness, the man who refuses to dilute himself becomes rare. And in a world of imitation, rarity is always irresistible.

U – Unshakable Standards (Application)

How Standards Attract: The Man Who Won't Settle **-** The man who refuses to settle always stands out. Not because he's louder or flashier than others, but because he moves differently — slower, steadier, more intentional. In a world addicted to instant gratification, he's not rushing. While others chase what's easy, he waits for what's aligned. His energy doesn't plead or perform. It holds. And people feel that — they feel the weight of a man who lives by choice rather than by chance.

When you live with unshakable standards, attraction becomes effortless. You stop trying to persuade others to see your value because your life already demonstrates it. Every decision — from the company you keep to how you spend your mornings — broadcasts your worth. You don't need to declare what you deserve; your consistency does the talking. And that is where quiet power begins.

Here's the truth most men miss: standards don't push people away; they filter them. Every time you enforce a boundary, you clarify your value. You separate the ones who drain your energy from the ones who elevate it. That filtration process might feel lonely at first — but it's sacred. Because attraction isn't about appealing to everyone; it's about resonating deeply with the few who recognize your frequency. The man who knows what he stands for doesn't need a crowd. He only needs alignment.

This is why the man who won't settle always draws attention. He's rare. Most people are used to negotiation — they expect you to lower your standards for convenience, to compromise your principles for approval. But when they encounter a man who calmly refuses, who can walk away without resentment, they feel something unfamiliar: respect. That respect is the seed of attraction. It's not about dominance or arrogance; it's about integrity. You become magnetic not because you're hard to get, but because you're hard to *shake*.

Women, especially, are drawn to this energy. When a man doesn't need her validation to feel valuable, her instincts recognize him as safe and strong. He's not swayed by beauty, mood, or manipulation. He appreciates her, but doesn't pedestalize her. He listens, but doesn't lose himself. His restraint creates polarity — a subtle, electric tension that draws her closer. Because she can feel that his attention is a privilege, not a reflex.

Imagine two men. One seeks constant approval, eager to please, bending his boundaries just to be liked. The other listens, smiles, but stays unmoved when tested. He doesn't match her emotional waves; he anchors them. He can say, "No, that doesn't work for me," with calm eyes and no apology. That moment — that quiet refusal — creates the attraction most men spend years chasing. Because women don't fall for compliance; they fall for conviction.

But standards don't just affect romance — they shape every interaction. In business, friendships, and social circles, the man who lives by a clear code is treated differently. His time is respected. His words carry more weight. His silence feels heavier. He doesn't need to control others to gain influence; his consistency creates its own gravity. When you hold a standard long enough, people start adjusting to meet it. That's leadership.

To embody this energy, you must understand that standards are not a list of demands — they're a way of life. You don't announce them; you express them through behavior. You respond slower, speak less, and let your boundaries do the talking. When something feels off, you don't explain for hours — you disengage. When someone crosses a line, you don't argue — you withdraw your energy. Your restraint becomes your loudest message. Because presence loses its power when it's overgiven.

Maintaining high standards requires emotional strength. You will be tested. People will call you distant, arrogant, or difficult. They'll project their discomfort because your self-respect exposes their lack of it. But you can't lower your frequency just to make others comfortable.

Standards are a mirror — they reflect your relationship with yourself. When you betray them, you don't just lose respect from others; you lose trust in your own judgment. But when you hold them — especially under pressure — your energy deepens. You start walking with quiet certainty, and that certainty becomes irresistible.

Standards are not about control; they're about clarity. You're not trying to manipulate outcomes — you're defining your parameters. When you know what you stand for, you move through the world like a man with purpose. You say less but mean more. You don't need to chase attention because your energy naturally commands it. You don't ask for respect; your boundaries demand it. And because you don't settle, everything that enters your life arrives with higher quality — people, opportunities, relationships.

There's a visible difference between a man who hopes and a man who expects. The one who hopes waits to be chosen. The one who expects knows he's the prize. That expectation isn't entitlement; it's alignment. It comes from years of honoring your word, following your code, and refusing to compromise your values for comfort. That's what creates the subtle, undeniable aura of authority — the kind that makes others straighten their posture when you walk into a room.

If you want to become that man, start with small acts of non-negotiation. Keep your word to yourself. Don't cancel your workout because you're tired. Don't entertain conversations that drain you. Don't chase attention when you could be building presence. These small boundaries are where your standards begin. Over time, they solidify into instinct. You stop needing to think about what to allow — your system already knows.

And when your life runs on standards rather than impulses, attraction stops being effortful. People sense the stability in your energy. Women feel it as safety and strength. Men recognize it as authority. The world sees it as confidence. You stop chasing validation because your life, your habits, your tone all communicate the same message: *I am not here to be liked. I am here to be respected.*

That's how standards attract — not through exclusion, but through elevation. You raise your life's frequency, and only those who match it can stay. You stop auditioning for others, and they start qualifying for you. The man who won't settle becomes the one everyone notices — not because he demands attention, but because he radiates something the modern world has almost forgotten: self-respect. When you live this way, attraction stops being something you pursue. It becomes something you *emit*.

L – Leadership (Concept)

Direction, Clarity, and Grounded Power - Every man is a leader — not because of position, but because of influence. The question isn't whether you lead; it's *what* you lead — chaos or order, fear or purpose, weakness or strength. Leadership begins the moment you stop waiting for permission and start taking responsibility for the direction of your life. It's not about commanding others; it's about commanding yourself. It's not about power over people; it's about power over your impulses. True leadership starts within — and until you've mastered that inner authority, every other form of leadership is just noise.

The modern man has been misled about leadership. He's been told it's about charisma, status, or dominance. He's seen it portrayed as loud, assertive, and constantly in motion. But real leadership is quiet. It's not the man who shouts the loudest who commands the room — it's the man whose stillness sets the rhythm for everyone else. True power doesn't need to broadcast itself; it's felt through certainty. When a man knows who he is and where he's going, people naturally align around him. Direction is magnetic because clarity is rare.

Leadership begins with direction — the ability to see clearly what others can't. Most people drift. They move through life reacting to whatever's in front of them, pulled by convenience and emotion. But the leader moves with intention. He's not driven by urgency; he's guided by vision. He knows what he wants, not because he's obsessed with control, but because he's connected to purpose. That connection gives his every action weight. You can see it in the way he walks, the way he speaks, the way he listens. Nothing feels random. His clarity radiates through his energy, and people sense it instinctively.

Clarity is one of the rarest currencies in the world. In a time where confusion is constant and opinions are endless, the man who speaks with direction stands out. Clarity doesn't mean knowing everything — it means knowing what matters. It's the ability to cut through noise and prioritize purpose. The leader doesn't need to chase validation because he already operates from alignment. He's not swayed by trends, moods, or approval. His compass is internal, not external. And because of that, he becomes unshakable.

Grounded power is what holds it all together. Power without grounding becomes tyranny; grounding without power becomes passivity. True masculine leadership lives in the balance — firm but flexible, confident but calm. A grounded leader is never reactive. He doesn't rise to every challenge with aggression, nor does he retreat at the first sign of conflict. He stands his ground — steady, composed, aware. His presence alone recalibrates the energy around him. When chaos erupts, people look to him instinctively, not because he demands it, but because his calm gives direction. That's leadership at its most primal level: stability in motion.

To lead others, you must first lead your emotions. You can't guide a team, a relationship, or a family if you can't guide yourself. The man who loses composure every time life tests him hasn't earned the right to lead. Leadership requires emotional discipline — the ability to stay centered when others lose balance. That's why grounded power is so magnetic. When everyone else is pulled by fear, you remain calm. When others hesitate, you act. When others panic, you think. That steadiness breeds trust. And trust is the foundation of all leadership — without it, influence is temporary.

But leadership is not about control; it's about containment. It's about holding space for others — for their emotions, for their confusion, for their growth — without being pulled into it. The strong leader doesn't suppress emotion; he directs it. He allows energy to move through him without letting it consume him. In relationships, this creates polarity — the feminine can express fully because the masculine doesn't crumble under her storm. In business, it creates confidence — teams move with clarity because the leader doesn't spread panic. In life, it creates peace — because your energy no longer rises and falls with external chaos.

Leadership also demands humility — the awareness that power is a responsibility, not a privilege. The best leaders don't seek followers; they create other leaders. They don't need to dominate; they inspire direction. They don't impose order; they embody it. Their authority doesn't come from ego but from example. That's why true leadership is attractive — it's the embodiment of integrity in motion. People crave stability, and the leader provides it simply by being anchored.

Women feel leadership before they ever hear it. It's not in the words you use; it's in the rhythm of your presence. When you walk into a room grounded and self-assured, when you speak slowly and listen fully, when you take responsibility instead of deflecting blame — she feels it. She feels that you know where you're going. That confidence allows her to relax into her own energy. Because leadership isn't about dominance; it's about direction. And direction, when it's clean and calm, creates safety.

Every man has leadership potential, but few develop it because it requires consistency. It requires facing yourself daily — your fears, your flaws, your patterns. It requires showing up even when no one's watching, making decisions when the path isn't clear, and trusting your instincts when doubt whispers louder than reason. Leadership is forged in those quiet moments of isolation, when it would be easier to follow but you choose to stand. That's when clarity turns into conviction.

The man who leads himself first becomes unstoppable. His power doesn't depend on position, wealth, or recognition. It lives in his character — in the way he handles pressure, treats people, and carries responsibility. When he speaks, his words have gravity because they come from experience, not ego. When he acts, he moves with purpose, not performance. His leadership isn't loud, but it's undeniable.

True leadership isn't built in moments of comfort. It's revealed in moments of chaos. When everything around you wavers, your steadiness becomes the anchor others cling to. And that's the essence of grounded power — not the ability to control the storm, but the ability to remain unmoved within it.

When a man learns to lead himself — his emotions, his energy, his standards — he naturally begins to lead everything around him. His presence becomes structure. His words become guidance. His silence becomes strength.

That's leadership: direction rooted in clarity, power balanced by humility, and confidence grounded in peace. Because in the end, leadership isn't about standing above others. It's about standing so firmly within yourself that others rise just by being near you.

L – Leadership (Application)

The Art of Quiet Command in Life, Love, and Presence - Leadership doesn't announce itself. You can't hear it in volume or see it in grand gestures. It shows itself in subtle ways — in the calm man who speaks last, in the one who listens longer, in the one who doesn't crumble when pressure rises. Quiet leadership is the rarest kind because it requires self-control instead of performance. It's not reactive, and it's not self-serving. It's rooted in awareness — the awareness of what needs to be done and the confidence to move first.

In social settings, quiet leadership reveals itself through rhythm. It's the man who naturally steers the energy of a room without forcing it. He doesn't demand attention; he organizes it. When conversations scatter, his voice grounds them. When tension rises, his humor softens it. When confusion lingers, his calm creates clarity. He never tries to dominate because true leaders never need to. His authority doesn't come from control — it comes from composure.

You can see it in the way he carries himself. When others rush to speak, he pauses. When others seek validation, he observes. He's not there to impress; he's there to direct energy. That's why people turn toward him instinctively — because he's steady in a world that moves too fast. Leadership in this sense isn't about charisma; it's about coherence. People gravitate toward whoever makes them feel most certain. And the calm man who doesn't react to noise becomes that source of certainty.

In daily life, leadership expresses itself through consistency. It's how you show up when no one's watching. The leader isn't defined by what he says, but by what he repeats — the morning routine he doesn't skip, the promises he keeps, the standards he lives by even when no one would notice if he didn't. His power doesn't depend on motivation. It lives in rhythm. Because leadership isn't about direction for others — it's about discipline for yourself. You can't guide anyone if you can't keep your own word.

The quiet leader doesn't lecture. He lives. He doesn't tell others what to do; he embodies what should be done. People feel the difference. In a culture where everyone talks about values, the man who simply *is* his values becomes magnetic. His discipline becomes visible in his body, his tone, his habits. He's not perfect, but he's consistent — and that consistency builds trust.

In relationships, leadership shows up as direction — not control, but guidance. A woman doesn't want to be managed; she wants to feel safe in your frame. She wants to sense that you can hold emotional storms without losing yourself. Quiet leadership here means being decisive without being domineering. It's saying, "We'll take care of this," instead of "What do we do?" It's listening fully, validating her feelings, and then leading the moment with clarity.

Leadership in romance isn't about making all the decisions; it's about providing stability through action. It's the simple things: making plans instead of waiting for her to, choosing a restaurant instead of asking endlessly, holding her hand confidently as you cross the street. It's subtle direction — the reassurance that you know where you're going, both physically and emotionally. That energy relaxes her nervous system. It allows her to soften, to trust, to express fully. Because deep down, she doesn't want control; she wants confidence.

Quiet leadership in love also means staying composed when emotion enters the room. When she tests you, challenges you, or expresses frustration, your reaction defines the dynamic. The weak man argues or retreats. The leader listens, breathes, and stays grounded. He doesn't match her chaos with chaos — he holds his calm. He allows her to express without collapsing. That's how emotional polarity is maintained. The feminine flows; the masculine contains. Leadership isn't about silencing her — it's about giving her space to be fully herself without losing yourself in the process.

In conflict, quiet leadership chooses direction over ego. When you're misunderstood, you clarify instead of defend. When others lose control, you maintain tone. You speak slowly, with measured rhythm, because you understand that tone leads emotion. The calmest energy in the room always wins — not through dominance, but through gravity. When you remain grounded while others spiral, people subconsciously defer to your steadiness. That's influence. That's leadership.

Even in small interactions — a negotiation, a disagreement, a moment of tension — quiet leadership looks the same: control of self before control of situation. You breathe deeper than everyone else. You speak with less rush. You move with precision. These are not performances; they're signals of mastery. They communicate, *I am not owned by this moment.* That steadiness disarms people. It earns respect without words.

Leadership also lives in humility. The quiet leader doesn't need to be right all the time. He admits when he's wrong, corrects course, and moves forward without drama. His ego is secondary to his mission. That humility doesn't weaken his power — it strengthens it. Because nothing is more commanding than a man who can hold both strength and accountability. People trust him because they sense that his direction isn't driven by pride, but by purpose.

And that's the essence of grounded leadership — purpose over performance. You lead not to be seen, but because direction is your nature. You lead not to control, but to stabilize. You lead not to impress, but to elevate. This is why quiet leaders are magnetic. They give more than they take, act more than they speak, and inspire more than they demand. Their influence extends beyond words — it lives in the energy they leave behind.

In truth, leadership is not something you switch on. It's something you become. It starts when you take responsibility for your energy — how you show up, how you react, how you guide others through uncertainty. You don't have to be in charge to lead. You only have to be *centered*.

When you live this way, everything you touch starts to move in rhythm with you. People breathe easier around you. Conversations slow down. Decisions come faster. Emotion settles. That's the subtle art of leadership — the transformation of space through presence. And when you embody that presence consistently, the world doesn't just notice you — it trusts you.

A – Attraction (Concept)

Polarity and the Psychology of Desire - Attraction isn't a choice. It's a response — an ancient, biological signal that happens before thought, before reason, before logic ever enters the room. You can't negotiate attraction, and you can't fake it. It lives in energy, not effort. It's the invisible tension between two opposing forces — the masculine and the feminine — pulling each other into balance. That's polarity. And when polarity is alive, desire follows naturally.

To understand attraction, you have to see it for what it really is: energetic alignment. The masculine and feminine are not genders — they're polar energies that exist within everyone. The masculine is direction, structure, presence, and depth. The feminine is flow, emotion, expression, and chaos. The masculine creates the container; the feminine fills it. The masculine penetrates through distraction; the feminine dances within sensation. When these energies meet — one steady, one alive — they create an electric current that can't be replicated through words or tactics.

A woman doesn't fall for how much you talk, how funny you are, or how impressive your achievements look on paper. She feels you before she hears you. Her body reads your energy faster than her mind processes your words. She notices how you breathe, how you look at her, how relaxed your shoulders are when she speaks. She's not reacting to your status; she's reacting to your state. Because her instincts are wired to sense safety and strength — not through protection, but through presence.

Presence is what keeps attraction alive. It's the signal that says, *I'm here. I see you. I'm not afraid of you, and I'm not trying to control you.* Most men think attraction is about dominance. It's not. Dominance without awareness is control, and control kills polarity. True masculine energy doesn't seek to suppress the feminine — it holds space for it. It doesn't fear her chaos; it stabilizes it. When a woman feels your calm presence while she's emotional, she relaxes into her feminine. When she feels your direction while she's uncertain, she softens into trust. When she feels your composure while she tests your strength, she feels safe enough to open. That's the essence of desire: safety that excites.

Polarity thrives on difference. The reason many modern relationships lose spark is because both energies collapse into sameness. The man becomes soft to avoid conflict; the woman becomes structured to compensate. Polarity dies when the masculine forgets to lead and the feminine forgets to flow. Desire doesn't survive in equality — it survives in complementarity. The feminine blooms in the presence of strength, and the masculine sharpens in the presence of openness. They don't compete; they complete the circuit.

But attraction also depends on tension — the subtle push and pull between stillness and motion, depth and expression. When a man is fully grounded, he becomes like gravity: steady, unmoved, drawing everything toward him without effort. The feminine responds to that gravity instinctively. She can relax because she can feel that he won't collapse. That doesn't mean she wants a man who controls her; she wants a man who can *contain* her — not physically, but emotionally. Containment isn't restriction; it's direction. It's the ability to hold her storms without drowning in them.

When you embody presence, a woman feels both safe and thrilled. Safe because your steadiness anchors her. Thrilled because your energy challenges her. It's the paradox that keeps desire alive — comfort with a pulse of danger. She wants to feel that you could lose control, but you choose not to. That choice — that calm command over your instincts — is what separates the attractive man from the forgettable one. The attractive man doesn't repress his hunger; he channels it. His desire isn't needy; it's directional. It's not, "Please choose me." It's, "I see you. And I choose you."

Attraction at its highest level isn't about external performance; it's about internal coherence. The masculine man attracts because he's integrated

— his mind, body, and energy move in the same rhythm. His intentions are clear, his emotions grounded, his words aligned with his presence. He doesn't need to convince; he simply embodies. The feminine, sensing that wholeness, relaxes. Her body and heart open in response to his grounded certainty. She's not reacting to charm — she's responding to integrity.

Attraction fades when men chase approval instead of alignment. Every time you try to impress, you subtly place her above you. You make her opinion your compass instead of your own purpose. And when your center shifts outside yourself, your energy weakens. The feminine doesn't follow weakness — not because she's cruel, but because her biology is designed to seek stability. The man who constantly needs reassurance can't provide the emotional leadership she craves. She might care for him, but she won't feel drawn to him. Desire and pity cannot coexist.

When a man reclaims his direction — when he stops reacting and starts leading — attraction rekindles. Not because he becomes harder, but because he becomes clearer. Clarity is masculine currency. The clearer you are about who you are, what you want, and what you stand for, the stronger your signal becomes. And the stronger your signal, the easier it is for the feminine to respond. She can feel where you're going, and that sense of direction pulls her toward you.

Attraction isn't something you create by effort. It's something you *allow* by alignment. You don't need to chase chemistry; you embody polarity. When you live in purpose, move with presence, and lead with calm authority, desire happens naturally. You don't need to manipulate her emotions or perform confidence — your grounded energy does all the talking.

The truth is, women don't fall for men who are flawless. They fall for men who are *anchored*. Men who can feel deeply but remain steady. Men who have direction but stay flexible. Men who carry power but don't abuse it. That balance between strength and stillness, depth and control, is what the feminine responds to on a primal level. It's not learned through tactics — it's remembered through embodiment. When your masculine energy is integrated, attraction stops being a pursuit. It becomes gravity. And gravity never chases — it pulls.

A – Attraction (Application)

Authentic Seduction: Communication, Confidence, and Subtle Dominance - Authentic seduction begins where performance ends. It's not about tricks, tactics, or memorized lines — it's about alignment. When your energy, your intention, and your expression all move in the same rhythm, you become naturally seductive without even trying. Seduction in its truest form isn't about getting someone to feel something; it's about allowing them to *feel you*. And that can only happen when you're fully present in your own body, calm in your energy, and rooted in truth.

You can't fake this. A woman can sense the difference between a man who's grounded and a man who's performing. When you're trying to impress, your energy leaks. Your tone tightens, your laughter sounds forced, your presence feels scattered. You might say all the right words, but she feels the hesitation behind them. Authentic seduction happens when you stop trying to be seductive. When your calm confidence replaces the need for validation, your energy shifts from seeking to offering — and that's what draws her in.

Communication is the foundation of that shift. But not the kind most men focus on — not clever words, not witty banter, not endless compliments. Real communication starts with presence. It's in the pauses between your words, the stillness in your gaze, the steadiness of your tone. You listen fully, without rushing to respond. You make eye contact without expectation. You hold silence comfortably. That's when attraction begins to thicken — when she feels your awareness wrapping around her like an invisible current. She's not responding to what you're saying; she's responding to how it feels to be seen by you.

A man who can communicate with presence becomes unforgettable. His attention isn't scattered; it's deliberate. When he asks a question, it's not out of politeness but genuine curiosity. When he speaks, his words carry weight because they come from stillness, not insecurity. He doesn't fill space with noise; he fills it with certainty. And in that space, the feminine feels something rare: safety and tension at the same time. She feels that he could take control at any moment — but he doesn't need to. That restraint is what makes his energy powerful.

Confidence, in this sense, is not about arrogance or perfection. It's about comfort in your own skin. It's the unspoken understanding that you don't need anything from her to feel valuable. When you walk into a room, you don't scan for approval — you bring energy with you. Your posture is relaxed, your movements slow, your presence steady. You're not performing confidence; you're embodying calm. Confidence is quiet, and quiet confidence is seductive. Because in a world of men who try too hard, the one who simply *is* becomes magnetic.

Confidence also lives in your boundaries. The seductive man doesn't over-pursue. He doesn't chase validation or force attention. He knows his value, and that knowing shapes his rhythm. When she pulls away, he doesn't panic. When she tests him, he doesn't react. His steadiness communicates everything his words don't need to. It tells her, *You can't shake me.* That emotional composure creates attraction far deeper than appearance ever could. Because desire lives in trust — and trust is born from consistency.

Then there's subtle dominance — the final layer of authentic seduction. This is not aggression or control; it's the natural expression of masculine leadership in intimacy. Subtle dominance is felt, not declared. It's the energy that says, *I can guide this moment, and I know you want me to.* It's in how you touch — slow, certain, intentional. It's in how you move — leading with quiet assurance, not demand. It's in how you hold her —

firmly enough to make her feel protected, gently enough to make her feel free.

Subtle dominance is direction expressed through presence. When you initiate touch, you don't ask for permission — you *read* it. You move when the energy calls for it, not when your anxiety needs reassurance. You understand that leadership in intimacy isn't about taking; it's about guiding. You don't dominate to overpower — you lead to create polarity. You give her the freedom to surrender by showing her that you can handle her energy without flinching. That's the essence of the masculine role in seduction: stillness that invites motion, certainty that awakens trust.

A woman's desire doesn't bloom through words; it blooms through contrast. She feels alive in the presence of a man who holds both restraint and power, who can tease with silence as effectively as with touch, who doesn't rush the moment but lets it unfold in rhythm. The man who understands this moves differently. He's playful, but never needy. He's teasing, but never cruel. He knows that seduction isn't about conquest — it's about connection. It's not about what he gets, but about what he creates: an experience where she feels fully feminine, fully seen, fully safe to express without judgment.

This is what most men never learn: seduction isn't something you do *to* her. It's something you create *with* her. It's a dance of energies — the masculine providing direction, the feminine responding with flow. The polarity between structure and surrender builds naturally when the masculine leads with awareness. When you lead from ego, she resists. When you lead from presence, she melts.

To live as an authentically seductive man, you must learn to trust the slow pace of tension. Don't rush it. Don't break the silence too soon. Don't try to "close the deal." The longer you can stay relaxed in uncertainty, the more she feels your strength. Every pause, every glance, every moment of stillness becomes a kind of foreplay — not physical, but energetic. You create desire by being completely unhurried, completely grounded, completely here.

Seduction, at its highest level, is not about getting a reaction — it's about evoking emotion. It's about leaving her with a feeling she can't shake, a calm excitement that lingers long after you've gone. You do that not by what you do, but by how you make her feel in your presence — seen, safe, desired, and unpressured. That balance of attention and detachment is the rarest energy in the world.

When you master communication through presence, confidence through self-trust, and subtle dominance through calm direction, attraction stops being something you chase. It becomes something you radiate. You stop needing to be "the bad boy" — because you've become something more powerful: a man who moves through the world with quiet authority and magnetic peace. That's authentic seduction: the art of making her feel deeply without saying much at all.

The Inner Empire: Self-Mastery

"The outer game sharpens your edge. The inner game shapes your world."

By now, you've felt the shift. Everything up to this point — the presence, the energy, the attraction — has been about the *outer edge* of your masculine power. How you move, how you lead, how you connect. The way your calm steadiness draws attention without effort. The way your composure in the face of chaos creates gravity.

But true mastery doesn't stop at the edge. It goes inward. The outer world is a reflection of your inner structure, and if that structure is weak — if your habits, your thoughts, and your emotions are undisciplined — your edge eventually dulls. Presence fades. Confidence fractures. Leadership turns performative. You can't hold external power for long if the internal foundation isn't built.

Most men never make this turn. They build the surface but neglect the core. They learn how to talk, how to walk, how to hold eye contact — but when life tests them, they crumble. Because what keeps a man solid isn't how he looks when things are smooth, but how he stands when everything shakes. The outer edge gives you magnetism; the inner empire gives you mastery.

The "bad boy" that the world romanticizes is only half the story. His rebellion, his presence, his allure — all of it begins to decay if it isn't rooted in discipline, direction, and purpose. Without those, confidence becomes chaos. Power becomes impulse. And freedom becomes emptiness. The man who has truly evolved beyond performance understands that the outer world is just an echo of what happens within. If you want to lead others, you must first lead yourself.

Self-mastery is not about control — it's about alignment. It's about making your thoughts, habits, and emotions serve your mission instead of sabotage it. It's the quiet, unseen process of refinement: waking up early when no one will praise you for it, keeping promises you made only to yourself, saying no to distractions that dull your focus. It's in those moments that your confidence stops being performance and becomes identity.

Because what you practice in silence becomes your energy in the world. The man who disciplines his mind doesn't need to prove his strength. It radiates from him naturally — in the way he listens, in the way he moves, in the way he decides. When your inner world is in order, your outer world organizes itself around it.

The next stage of your evolution isn't about adding — it's about *subtracting*. Removing the habits, distractions, and patterns that keep you from being fully present. Replacing chaos with rhythm, weakness with structure, and noise with purpose. That's where power deepens.

The outer game sharpens your edge. But the inner game shapes your world. You've learned to command attention. Now it's time to command yourself. To build the kind of discipline that becomes freedom. To develop the kind of peace that becomes power. To create the kind of man who doesn't just attract — he *embodies*. Once you've mastered how to move through the world, the next question becomes: Can you master how you move within yourself? Because that's where real confidence is born. That's where your empire begins.

The Discipline Code (Concept)

Discipline has been misunderstood. To most men, it sounds like a cage — a series of rules that strangle freedom, a life stripped of spontaneity and pleasure. But real discipline isn't a prison; it's protection. It's the structure that holds your freedom in place. The undisciplined man is not free — he's a slave to impulse, emotion, and distraction. The disciplined man isn't restricted — he's liberated from chaos.

True discipline isn't about denying yourself; it's about directing yourself. It's the daily act of devotion to the man you're becoming. Every routine, every repetition, every refusal to compromise on your standards is a way of saying: *I remember who I am.* Discipline is not punishment for who you were — it's preparation for who you're becoming.

The modern world has made consistency seem boring, as if routine were the enemy of passion. But in truth, consistency is what builds power. Every time you follow through — when you do what you said you would, even when no one's watching — you're carving identity into your nervous system. Each small act of discipline becomes a vote for the man you believe yourself to be. Eventually, those votes become certainty. And certainty is the root of confidence.

Consistency forges identity because it builds trust within yourself. Most men break that trust daily — they promise themselves change but never follow through. They talk about goals but live in excuses. Over time, that inconsistency corrodes their self-belief. Every broken promise whispers the same message: *You can't rely on yourself.* And when a man can't rely on himself, he starts reaching outward for validation, control, or distraction. That's why discipline isn't about external performance — it's about restoring inner credibility.

The disciplined man doesn't need to prove anything, because he's built proof through action. His word means something — first to himself, then to others. When he says he'll do something, his body already knows it's true. That quiet reliability creates the kind of power that can't be faked. People feel it when he speaks. They sense the integrity beneath his calm. His energy doesn't fluctuate with mood or motivation because his identity is built on consistency, not emotion.

Discipline isn't about grinding yourself into exhaustion; it's about alignment. When your habits match your values, you stop fighting yourself. You stop negotiating with laziness, overthinking, and impulse. Your daily rituals — how you move, eat, speak, train, and rest — become reflections of your standards. You no longer need to chase motivation because rhythm replaces it. The disciplined man doesn't wait to feel ready; he acts because readiness is irrelevant. Action comes first, and feeling follows.

What makes discipline powerful is that it's internal. No one can give it to you, and no one can take it away. You can lose money, relationships, or opportunity — but if you've built discipline, you'll rebuild everything else. Because discipline is the one skill that transcends circumstance. It's how you prove to yourself that no external condition determines your inner direction. That's why discipline, at its highest form, is not about control — it's about faith.

Faith in your mission. Faith in your process. Faith in the unseen man you're building with every repetition.

When discipline becomes devotion, it transforms your energy. The world can feel the difference between a man who trains because he hates himself and a man who trains because he honors himself. One is driven by insecurity; the other by reverence. Discipline rooted in devotion gives your life gravity. It gives your presence weight. Because devotion is love expressed through consistency — love for your craft, your potential, your future self.

And that's what most men are missing: love disguised as structure. The structure that makes space for their greatness to emerge. The average man runs from discipline because he thinks it kills joy. But what it really kills is chaos — and in that quiet, joy finally has room to breathe.

Discipline doesn't demand perfection. It demands return. You'll stumble. You'll drift. You'll fall short. But the difference between the lost man and the disciplined man is that the disciplined one always returns to center. Every time he gets off course, he comes back faster. That return is what sharpens him. That return is what keeps him grounded. Over time, he becomes the kind of man who doesn't need to find motivation — he *is* motivation.

Consistency is the proof of identity. You don't become disciplined by telling yourself you will be; you become disciplined by acting disciplined one day at a time. Every repetition of action etches a line of certainty into your character until one day, you don't have to think about it anymore. You wake up early because that's who you are. You train because that's who you are. You follow through because that's who you are. Discipline stops being something you do — it becomes something you *are*.

That's when a man truly becomes powerful: when he no longer needs to convince himself to do what must be done. His habits have become his home. His actions, his prayer. His consistency, his language of devotion.

Discipline, at its highest level, is freedom disguised as routine. It's the invisible rhythm that keeps your energy grounded when the world pulls you in every direction. It's what allows you to move through life with clarity, confidence, and calm — because you've already proven to yourself that you'll do what needs to be done, no matter what. And that's the secret of the inner empire: Discipline isn't the sacrifice of freedom. It's how freedom is earned.

The Discipline Code (Application)

There comes a point in every man's journey where discipline stops feeling like effort and starts feeling like flow. It's no longer a struggle between who you are and who you want to be — the two finally meet. What used to feel heavy becomes light. The habits that once felt forced become instinct. The mornings you used to dread become sacred. The structure you once resisted becomes the very thing that makes you feel alive.

That's the moment when discipline turns into freedom — when your rhythm becomes your release.

At first, it's hard. Discipline always begins as resistance. You drag yourself out of bed before the world wakes. You push through fatigue when your body screams for comfort. You say no when temptation calls your name. It feels like punishment, like constant self-denial. But over time, something subtle happens. The pain of discipline transforms into the peace of order. You start craving the structure that once felt restrictive. The repetition that used to feel monotonous begins to give you strength. Each small act of control — each completed task, each kept promise — adds another layer of clarity to your mind.

And then, one day, you wake up and realize you don't need motivation anymore. You move because movement is who you are. You act without debate, train without hesitation, focus without force. You've stopped negotiating with yourself. You've stopped asking whether you "feel like it." You do it because it's part of your nature now. That's when discipline becomes identity. And identity — the certainty of who you are — is the purest form of freedom.

Most men spend their lives chasing freedom by avoiding structure, not realizing that true freedom only exists within it. The man who wakes whenever he wants, eats whatever he wants, scrolls endlessly, and indulges every impulse isn't free — he's trapped in the prison of his desires. He's ruled by comfort. The man with discipline, on the other hand, moves through his day with quiet control. His schedule doesn't confine him; it liberates him from distraction. He doesn't need to fight his impulses because he's already decided who wins that battle. His decisions are made before temptation arrives. That's freedom — not the absence of rules, but the mastery of choice.

Discipline becomes flow when resistance disappears. Flow isn't mystical; it's mechanical. It's what happens when your preparation meets your purpose. It's when you've built such a strong relationship with discomfort that you stop fearing it. You know exactly how your body feels when it resists — and you move anyway. You know how your mind tries to escape — and you stay present anyway. Over time, this quiet defiance hardens into confidence. You stop fighting the waves and start surfing them. The friction that used to exhaust you now fuels you.

You can feel it in your body when you've reached this stage. Your mornings have rhythm. Your breath moves evenly. Your focus stays anchored. You're not rushing toward goals — you're flowing toward them. You no longer rely on hype or urgency; your momentum comes from consistency. Even your silence feels strong, because it's built on self-control.

When discipline matures into flow, life becomes simpler. You stop overcomplicating progress. You realize that mastery isn't about constant intensity; it's about sustained consistency. It's the small repetitions that shape the man — the early morning routine, the steady workouts, the mindful meals, the deliberate focus. You start to see your daily rituals as acts of reverence, not chores. Each repetition becomes a declaration: *I'm still here. I'm still moving. I still honor my potential.*

And that's what freedom feels like — not the absence of responsibility, but the ability to carry it lightly. You stop craving escape because you've found peace in the process. You don't need a vacation from your own life anymore. You've built a rhythm that restores you. You feel strong, not from adrenaline, but from harmony.

There's a moment that every disciplined man experiences — maybe during a morning run, maybe at the gym, maybe while working late when everyone else has gone home — when his mind goes quiet. No resistance, no noise, just presence. That's the flow state discipline was always leading you toward. You feel connected to something bigger than yourself — the pulse of purpose moving through your veins. It's not excitement; it's peace. Not intensity; balance. That's when you understand that discipline was never about control — it was about surrender. Surrendering to the process, to the rhythm, to the man you were always meant to become.

The man who reaches this point walks differently. He carries an aura of stability that others feel instantly. He doesn't need to boast about his routines or his grind. He's beyond proving. His actions speak quietly but consistently, and that quiet consistency becomes magnetic. People can sense that he's not trying to control life — he's in rhythm with it.

That's the paradox of discipline: what begins as effort ends as ease. The same structure that once felt heavy now carries you effortlessly. You realize that freedom was never found in avoiding responsibility — it was found in mastering it.

And so discipline, once misunderstood as a burden, becomes your sanctuary. It's the place where your chaos finds calm, where your mind finds stillness, and where your potential finds form. The man who understands this doesn't crave motivation anymore. He lives in motion. He doesn't chase freedom — he *is* freedom, refined through rhythm and anchored in devotion.

Because when discipline becomes your default, the world can no longer control you. And that's the highest form of liberty there is.

The Inner Voice (Concept)

Every man carries two voices inside him. The first is quiet but steady — it comes from the center. It knows. It doesn't shout or explain; it simply directs. The second is louder, faster, and uncertain — it questions, hesitates, negotiates. That second voice is the saboteur. It sounds like logic, but it's fear disguised as reason. It speaks in the language of safety, and it's responsible for killing more dreams, more confidence, and more attraction than failure ever could.

Self-doubt doesn't always roar. Most of the time, it whispers. *What if you're wrong? What if you're not ready? What if they don't like you?* It shows up the moment before action — the half-second pause that breaks your momentum, the quiet hesitation that makes your voice shake when it should be firm. It infects posture, tone, and energy long before words are spoken. And that's how it kills charisma.

Charisma isn't about charm or looks — it's about certainty. It's the invisible current of conviction that moves through your body and communicates: *I trust myself.* When that trust is fractured, people feel it instantly. Your energy falters. You second-guess. You seek approval before you've even spoken. The world reads it before you realize you're showing it. Women sense it faster than anyone — because her biology is tuned to feel uncertainty in a man's energy. The moment your inner voice turns from leadership to insecurity, polarity collapses.

Self-doubt is seductive because it pretends to protect you. It convinces you that hesitation equals intelligence — that second-guessing means you're being smart. But in truth, self-doubt is not caution; it's self-betrayal. It's the internal retreat from your own power. Every time you obey it, you reinforce weakness. You teach yourself to believe your fear more than your instinct. And over time, that becomes habit. You stop trusting your impulses. You stop taking risks. You start shrinking your life to fit your comfort zone.

The tragedy is that most men think their problem is external — they blame circumstances, rejection, timing. But their real obstacle is internal noise. You can't project confidence when you're at war with yourself. You can't lead others when you don't believe your own direction. And you can't be magnetic when your energy is diluted by doubt. Charisma, like attraction, begins with alignment. When your inner voice is divided, your presence fractures. When it's unified, everything you do carries weight.

That's why mastering the inner voice is not about silencing fear — it's about shifting authority. The goal isn't to eliminate doubt; it's to stop letting it lead. You don't need to argue with the saboteur; you simply stop taking orders from it. You let the deeper voice — the grounded, calm one — take command again. The one that speaks from instinct, not anxiety. The one that doesn't care who's watching.

You've felt that voice before — in moments of flow, in moments of danger, in moments where you stopped thinking and simply *knew*. It's the voice that moves before words, that acts without apology. That's your real self — the part of you that existed before conditioning, before overthinking, before you learned to perform. The more you trust it, the louder it becomes. The more you hesitate, the quieter it gets.

Self-doubt kills charisma because it breaks rhythm. Charisma isn't created — it's felt when energy flows freely. When you're second-guessing yourself, your energy stutters. You move in fragments — unsure tone, uncertain eyes, inconsistent energy. But when you trust your instinct fully, your energy moves in one smooth line. It's cohesive. It's confident. It's contagious. That's what people call *charisma* — coherence between thought, emotion, and action.

Most men think they need to speak perfectly to be charismatic. They don't. What matters isn't what you say — it's how much of you is behind it. You could say one sentence with full alignment and command the room, or speak for ten minutes with doubt and be forgotten. Charisma lives in certainty, not eloquence. And that certainty is born from silence — the inner stillness where your true voice can rise above the noise.

When you start to listen carefully, you'll notice that the inner saboteur always sounds urgent. It speaks in anxiety, speed, and scarcity. It rushes. It wants reaction, not reflection. The real inner voice is calm. It's grounded, measured, slow. It never pushes — it pulls. It doesn't promise safety, but it guarantees truth. You can feel the difference in your body. Doubt tightens your chest; direction relaxes it. Doubt creates tension; clarity creates stillness.

The practice of mastering your inner voice begins with awareness. You have to hear the lie before you can disobey it. You start noticing how often that voice tries to control you — in conversation, in hesitation, in every moment you withhold your truth to avoid discomfort. And each time you notice it, you have a choice: follow the saboteur or follow the signal.

When you start choosing instinct over insecurity, the world changes. You stop overexplaining. You stop apologizing for existing. You stop asking questions you already know the answer to. You start moving from a place of knowing rather than needing. That's when charisma begins to return — not as performance, but as presence.

Because charisma isn't about what you *do* to others; it's about what you *stop doing* to yourself. When you stop interrupting your own flow, your natural power re-emerges. People feel it. Women feel it. The room feels it. It's not that you've learned new tricks — it's that you've stopped getting in your own way.

Every man must face the saboteur within — that quiet enemy who thrives in hesitation. But once you see it for what it is, it loses control. Because you realize it's not your enemy at all — it's just the shadow of unclaimed power. It's the echo of every moment you doubted your worth. And when you finally turn toward it — not to fight, but to understand — it quiets.

That's when you hear the other voice again — the calm one. The one that doesn't ask for permission. The one that doesn't fear silence. The one that doesn't need to prove anything. That's your real leadership. That's your real charisma. And it's been waiting for you to listen.

The Inner Voice (Application)

The thinking man is praised. The decisive man is followed. The overthinking man is forgotten. Most men don't fail because they lack intelligence or intention. They fail because they live in hesitation — trapped between knowing and doing, between potential and proof. Overthinking is the most common form of self-sabotage because it disguises itself as preparation. You tell yourself you're being careful, strategic, responsible. But behind every delayed action hides the same truth: fear. Fear of judgment, fear of rejection, fear of being seen trying and not being perfect.

The only way to silence that fear is not by thinking harder — it's by moving anyway. Because clarity doesn't come from thought; it comes from experience.

Action is how you build trust with yourself. Every time you take a step — even a small one — you send your nervous system a message: *I move when I decide.* That message rewires your self-image. You start to see yourself as a man who acts, not hesitates. That's how confidence is created — not through affirmations, but through evidence. The more proof you create through action, the quieter your doubt becomes.

You've probably felt it before: the paralysis that comes from living too long in your head. You replay scenarios, calculate outcomes, craft perfect responses — all while life keeps moving without you. Overthinking makes you feel like you're in control, but really, it's just fear wearing a mask of logic. You're not preparing — you're avoiding. And avoidance is how potential rots.

A man who trusts himself doesn't need all the answers before he moves. He moves because he knows he'll adapt once he does. That's what separates confidence from arrogance. The arrogant man believes he can't fail; the confident man knows he can, but moves anyway. He understands that feedback — not fantasy — is the path to growth. Every action, even the imperfect ones, becomes information that sharpens his intuition.

You don't eliminate overthinking by fighting it. You replace it with motion. You teach your mind that thinking without doing is a dead loop. The moment you feel that spiral begin — that mental noise, that flood of what-ifs — is your cue to act. Make the call. Send the message. Lift the weight. Take the step. It doesn't matter how small; what matters is that you break the inertia. Because every time you act despite uncertainty, you reclaim authority over your mind.

Self-trust is built through rhythm. When you consistently act on your instincts — when you stop second-guessing your intuition — your energy becomes cohesive. Your body and mind start to operate as one. That's when presence deepens. That's when charisma returns. Because people can feel the difference between a man who's certain of his energy and a man who's trapped in his thoughts. The first moves with grace. The second twitches with tension.

This is why women are drawn to men who act with quiet decisiveness. It's not about dominance — it's about clarity. When a man moves with confidence, she can feel that he trusts himself. And that trust invites her to trust him too. You don't need to be perfect; you just need to be sure enough to lead. The energy of "I'll handle it" is infinitely more attractive than "I'm still thinking about it."

Action also neutralizes anxiety. Anxiety thrives in inactivity — it feeds on imagination. When you sit still and think, your mind starts to build monsters that don't exist. But when you move, you shrink them. You give your mind real data instead of speculation. You shift from victim to participant, from fear to flow.

Here's the truth: you'll never think your way into self-trust. You'll only act your way into it. Every decision you follow through on, every challenge you take head-on, every uncomfortable truth you confront —

all of it builds a track record. Over time, that track record becomes your confidence. You don't need to *believe* you can — you'll *know* you can, because you've done it before.

This is how a man becomes dangerous in peace — when he no longer hesitates. He doesn't rush, but he doesn't stall. His movements are deliberate. His words are chosen. His timing is impeccable — not because he's psychic, but because he's practiced. He's trained himself to trust his instincts through repetition. And repetition builds rhythm. Rhythm builds trust. Trust builds power. When you stop overthinking, life becomes simpler. You start seeing opportunities instead of obstacles. You stop waiting for motivation, because the act of movement creates it. You realize that confidence is not a prerequisite for action — it's the result of it. And once you understand that, you stop waiting to feel ready.

Action-based self-trust is the most masculine form of meditation. It grounds you in reality. It brings you out of your head and into the present moment — into the body, into breath, into now. Every time you act, you remind yourself that you are not a spectator in your life. You're the author. And the man who moves, writes.

So start small. Act before you're sure. Say what you mean. Follow through on the little things. Keep the promises no one else sees. Over time, the noise fades. The hesitation quiets. The voice of the saboteur weakens.

Because your nervous system learns the truth: You are not fragile. You are capable. You can trust yourself. And when a man truly trusts himself, the world begins to trust him too. That's when the inner voice no longer sabotages — it serves. It stops questioning your power and starts echoing it. That's when you stop performing confidence and start radiating it. And that's the beginning of real self-mastery.

The Warrior and the Monk

Every man is born with two instincts: the will to conquer and the need to be still. One seeks to expand, to push, to break through barriers and claim new ground. The other seeks to center — to understand, to breathe, to find harmony in the midst of chaos. These two forces — the warrior and the monk — live inside every man. But only the rare few learn how to let them coexist.

Most men are stuck on one side. The modern "warrior" burns himself out chasing dominance — he confuses aggression for power, busyness for purpose, tension for control. His strength becomes frantic, his energy sharp but unstable. On the other side, the "monk" retreats too deeply into peace — detached from the pulse of life, mistaking passivity for enlightenment. He may be calm, but his calm is empty. True mastery lives between them — in the man who can fight when necessary but is not ruled by the need to.

The warrior gives you edge; the monk gives you depth. One teaches you how to win, the other how to remain unshaken whether you win or lose. Together, they forge the kind of presence that commands respect without ever demanding it. Because the man who carries both strength and stillness in his body moves differently. He's aware of his power, but he doesn't need to prove it. His calm is not weakness — it's control. His silence is not passivity — it's precision.

The modern world worships noise — constant motion, endless opinions, exaggerated displays of confidence. But the man who embodies both the warrior and the monk doesn't play that game. He doesn't shout; he listens. He doesn't rush; he observes. He doesn't seek validation; he emits certainty. And that stillness unnerves people — because it's the energy of someone who cannot be manipulated. You can't provoke him, because his power doesn't live in reaction. It lives in restraint.

The warrior gives you the courage to act. The monk gives you the wisdom to wait. When they work together, your energy becomes lethal in its precision. You stop swinging wildly at every challenge; you start choosing your battles with intention. You move with purpose, not impulse. You no longer burn energy on proving yourself, because your presence already speaks louder than effort ever could.

To live as both warrior and monk is to understand rhythm — the ability to shift between fire and stillness at will. You train hard, but rest deeply. You fight fiercely, but forgive quickly. You speak directly, but never reactively. Your aggression becomes conscious, your stillness deliberate. That balance is rare, and that rarity is magnetic. People can feel when a man has mastered his polarity — when he can carry danger in his eyes and peace in his tone.

This is what calm dominance looks like. It's not the man who controls others, but the one who controls himself so completely that others naturally defer to his energy. His confidence doesn't need to rise above anyone; it simply stands unmoved. The calm man is not boring — he's terrifying to the insecure. Because calmness implies control, and control implies competence. When chaos hits, the loud ones panic. The calm one calculates. His stillness becomes strategy. His presence becomes leadership.

In a world obsessed with reacting, calmness is rebellion. It's power disguised as peace. You can feel it in a man who has truly integrated his warrior and monk — he walks with quiet readiness, the kind of energy that says, *I am prepared for peace, but capable of war.* You'll see it in his eyes — steady, focused, aware. You'll hear it in his voice — slow, measured, deliberate. When he speaks, he doesn't compete for space. He *creates* space.

That's the paradox of true dominance: the less you need to display power, the more people feel it. The man who yells to command is weak; the man who whispers and is still obeyed has presence. That's not performance

— it's calibration. You've mastered your nervous system so completely that your energy dictates the rhythm of the room. You become gravity. And gravity never chases.

Women feel this immediately. The man who has both fire and stillness awakens a deep instinct in her — she feels safe, yet alert. His energy says: *you are free here, but you are not leading.* He doesn't need to chase, nor does he resist connection. He allows it to flow toward him, then directs it with quiet authority. His calm invites her emotion. His steadiness invites her softness. His balance creates her surrender.

That's what makes the integration of warrior and monk so powerful in attraction and life alike. You are not just strong — you are *centered*. You are not just calm — you are *capable*. You can love deeply without losing yourself, fight fiercely without losing control, and lead powerfully without ego.

The warrior within you says, *I will not be defeated.* The monk within you whispers, *I don't need to fight.* Together, they form the man who is free.

Because power without peace destroys itself, and peace without power disappears. But when a man unites them, he becomes untouchable — a storm and a sanctuary in one frame.

That's the rarest energy on earth. The calm man who can go to war if needed. The dangerous man who chooses not to. The master who doesn't need to prove mastery. That's the new archetype of masculine dominance — not volume, not violence, but stillness. Because calm is not the absence of power. It's what power looks like once it's fully under control.

Purpose Over Pleasure

Every man must choose his master. For some, it's pleasure. For others, it's purpose. One consumes you; the other completes you.

Pleasure whispers promises of escape — a quick dopamine hit, a scroll, a drink, a night, a release. It tells you that you've earned it, that you deserve to rest, that comfort is the reward for effort. But pleasure is deceptive. It doesn't ask for much at first — only your attention. Then your consistency. Then your hunger. Eventually, it takes your edge.

Purpose, on the other hand, never seduces. It summons. It doesn't lure you with ease; it calls you into responsibility. It's the quiet voice that doesn't promise happiness but demands honesty. And if you answer it, your entire life begins to change — because you stop seeking stimulation and start building momentum.

The world has made pleasure too easy. You can consume more in one day than your ancestors could in a lifetime — content, connection, gratification, illusion. Comfort has become the cage that men voluntarily walk into. We've mistaken abundance for progress and indulgence for peace. But when everything is available instantly, meaning evaporates. Desire becomes dull.

That's why so many men feel numb even when life looks full. Pleasure without purpose is noise without rhythm. It gives you sensation but robs you of satisfaction. You get the high without the height. The result? A restless man — overstimulated, underfulfilled, always hungry but never fed.

The only cure for that hunger is mission. Mission gives a man gravity. It makes him dangerous again — not because he's violent, but because he's focused. A man on a mission doesn't need to escape himself, because he's anchored in something bigger than himself. His pleasure stops being random; it becomes earned. It becomes sacred.

Purpose isn't always glamorous. It's repetitive, demanding, and sometimes lonely. But within that repetition, you rediscover yourself. You stop drifting. You start building. You feel tension return to your body — not the tension of anxiety, but the tension of direction. The edge you lost in comfort sharpens again. The fire you thought was gone reignites. And suddenly, you're not searching for motivation — you *are* motivation.

When a man reconnects with purpose, everything else begins to align. His habits fall into place because they now have context. His discipline becomes devotion. His silence becomes strategy. Even his relationships change, because he's no longer trying to fill a void — he's leading from fullness.

And women feel this. They can sense when a man is driven by mission instead of need. Purpose gives a man depth. It turns attraction from chemistry into gravity. When she looks at a man with direction, she doesn't just see confidence — she feels safety. His presence tells her that he's not lost in the noise, that his attention is not scattered, that his energy has a destination.

The man on a mission doesn't chase validation because he's already fulfilled in pursuit. He doesn't collapse under emotion because his focus is anchored. He doesn't get thrown off balance by rejection, because his worth isn't on the line — his work is. That kind of grounded direction doesn't repel women; it magnetizes them. Because true feminine energy wants to flow into a frame that can hold it.

Purpose doesn't kill pleasure. It refines it. Pleasure, when aligned with purpose, becomes richer — a moment of reward, not escape. A man who lives for pleasure alone burns out in indulgence. A man who lives for purpose finds peace even in struggle. His satisfaction comes not from comfort, but from growth.

That's why mission must come before meaning, and meaning before indulgence. Because when a man forgets his mission, his energy fragments. He starts chasing excitement instead of expansion. But when he's on purpose, his energy unifies. He becomes calm in direction, patient in pursuit, and lethal in focus.

You can always feel the difference between a man who wakes up for pleasure and one who wakes up for purpose. One hits snooze. The other rises in silence. One looks for distraction. The other looks for challenge. One seeks validation. The other seeks mastery.

Purpose gives structure to a man's life the way a spine gives shape to a body. Without it, everything collapses inward. You lose posture, presence, clarity. But once you have it, everything stands taller — your habits, your relationships, your confidence. You move through the world differently. Every step carries intention. Every silence has weight.

A man with purpose is unshakable. Because he knows why he's here. He knows what he's building. He's not pulled by the winds of emotion or trend — he's rooted in his own direction. That kind of man doesn't need to shout to be heard. His actions echo louder than words ever could.

And here's the paradox: the more you give yourself to purpose, the more peace you feel. Because the restless energy that once sought escape now finds expression. The same passion that once burned you out now fuels you. Pleasure no longer drains you — it restores you. You stop chasing the next hit of stimulation because your life itself becomes stimulating.

Purpose is not the absence of pleasure. It's the mastery of it. It's knowing that real pleasure doesn't come from escape, but from engagement. It's the satisfaction of doing hard things well, of creating something lasting, of living in alignment with who you were built to be.

That's what liberation feels like — not the freedom to do whatever you want, but the power to direct yourself toward what truly matters. And when a man lives that way — when every move, every breath, every choice is tethered to a mission — he becomes something rare: peaceful, focused, magnetic. The kind of man who doesn't need to chase pleasure, because purpose makes pleasure chase him.

Mastery in Relationships

When a man builds his inner empire — when his thoughts, habits, and direction finally fall into rhythm — something subtle but profound begins to happen: his relationships change. Not because he learns new tactics or speaks differently, but because his energy no longer leaks. His world feels ordered, his presence grounded, his silence purposeful.

People feel that before he ever says a word.

When your world is aligned, connection stops being something you chase and becomes something you *create*. You stop needing others to complete you because you've already met yourself. You no longer enter relationships from hunger, but from fullness. And that changes everything — because attraction, at its core, is energy exchange. The more complete you are, the more space you give for real intimacy to grow.

Most men try to build connection from the outside in — through charm, performance, or strategy. But true connection begins from the inside out. It's the natural byproduct of internal clarity. When you're grounded in who you are, you don't grasp for attention or validation. You simply stand — steady, certain, unhurried — and the right energy gravitates toward you.

You've done the inner work. You've faced the noise, the hesitation, the indulgence, the emptiness. You've built structure where chaos once ruled. You've learned that peace isn't weakness, that presence is power, and that purpose is freedom.Now, you carry that power into every interaction — not as armor, but as gravity.

Because self-mastery isn't the end of the journey; it's the beginning of influence. The man who knows himself deeply leads others naturally. His energy draws respect, his stillness invites trust, and his direction gives those around him something to align with. That's where the next evolution begins: learning to translate your internal mastery into external connection — with women, with friends, with the world itself.

Polarity and Power

Attraction isn't an accident. It's alignment — two opposing energies finding rhythm. Masculine and feminine are not roles, but forces. They exist beyond gender, beyond personality, beyond culture. They are nature itself — the tide and the shore, the sun and the moon, the current and the container. And when they meet in full expression, the air changes. There's charge. There's tension. There's life.

Polarity is the heartbeat of attraction. It's what creates the spark that turns ordinary interaction into chemistry. Without it, connection fades. Relationships flatten. Desire dies quietly under comfort. Polarity isn't about dominance or submission — it's about the complementary dance between presence and expression. The masculine gives direction; the feminine gives flow. One stabilizes, the other expands. One holds, the other moves.

Masculine energy at its core is consciousness — awareness, structure, stillness. It's the grounded presence that says, *I am here. I know where I'm going.* Feminine energy is movement — emotion, intuition, creativity. It's the flow that says, *I feel, I express, I respond.* When these two meet in balance, attraction feels effortless. She feels safe to surrender, and he feels inspired to lead.

But when polarity collapses, attraction fades. You can feel it in modern relationships — a world that preaches equality but confuses it with sameness. Men are told to soften; women are told to harden. The result? Two energies trying to meet in the middle but finding no spark. Because chemistry doesn't live in comfort — it lives in contrast. It's the tension between his calm and her chaos, his direction and her expression, his silence and her storm, that creates the pulse of attraction.

Polarity is ancient. Before words, before rules, it's how energy recognized itself. In nature, you see it everywhere — the tree rooted in stillness and the wind dancing through its branches. The mountain unmoved, the river in motion. Neither is superior; both are necessary. The masculine without the feminine is rigid and cold. The feminine without the masculine is scattered and lost. Together, they create balance — form and flow, containment and freedom, logic and emotion, discipline and surrender.

The problem is, the modern world has made men forget their side of the dance. Masculinity has been domesticated — told to be agreeable, to emote without grounding, to yield its structure for approval. And when a man abandons his polarity, he loses the ability to attract. Not because women want "bad boys," but because they crave *direction*. They crave the masculine energy that allows them to relax into their own feminine nature.

When a woman says, "I just want to feel safe," she doesn't mean protected from danger — she means safe to express herself fully without fear of destabilizing the man in front of her. She wants to know that his center won't crumble under her emotion. That his stillness can hold her movement. That his calm is stronger than her storm. And when she feels that, something ancient awakens — respect, attraction, surrender. Not forced, not taught — felt.

Masculine power, when aligned, isn't control; it's containment. It's the ability to hold space for intensity without collapsing into it. That's why presence is so magnetic — it's the rarest form of safety. When a man can remain calm in the face of feminine energy — her laughter, her chaos, her emotion, her testing — he activates the deepest polarity. Because in that calm, she feels something she can trust: a man who won't run from her fullness.

This is what sustains attraction beyond the first spark. Looks may catch attention, but polarity keeps desire alive. It's not built on constant excitement but on energetic truth. When the masculine stays anchored and the feminine stays expressive, the current between them never dies. They challenge each other without breaking. They move between chaos and calm like a breath — tension and release, pursuit and surrender.

True polarity isn't about playing parts. It's about embodying essence. It's about remembering who you are and allowing her to do the same. When you lead with strength and peace, she responds with emotion and life. When you meet her storm with stillness, she softens. When you hold direction, she expands in trust. The more deeply you embody your masculine energy, the more freely she can express her feminine energy. And that exchange — that flow between groundedness and expression — is the pulse of desire itself.

This is why presence is the cornerstone of masculine power. Because without presence, polarity collapses. Without direction, the feminine drifts. Without containment, emotion overwhelms. But when you bring your full awareness into the moment — when your body, mind, and energy are aligned — she feels it instantly. The room changes. The conversation deepens. Her body relaxes, her guard lowers, her eyes soften. She's not responding to your words — she's responding to your *energy*.

Polarity doesn't need to be forced. It simply needs to be remembered.

When you stop trying to be liked and start standing in truth, you reclaim your role in the dance. You become the still point around which everything moves — calm, focused, certain. And in that certainty, attraction stops being performance and becomes nature again.

Charisma and Connection

There's a certain kind of man who walks into a room and doesn't need to say much. He's not the loudest or the most polished. He doesn't use clever lines or chase reactions. Yet somehow, people turn toward him. They feel drawn — not to his words, but to his *energy*. That's charisma in its purest form: not performance, but presence.

Most men mistake charm for charisma. Charm is the art of pleasing; charisma is the art of being. Charm manipulates perception; charisma radiates truth. Charm works when you're trying to win approval. Charisma begins when you stop needing it.

Charm is external — a mask designed to create effect. It's how you tilt your head, time your laugh, control your image. It can impress people, even seduce them for a moment. But it can't hold their attention for long, because it depends on constant effort. The moment you stop performing, the illusion breaks.

Authenticity, by contrast, is magnetic precisely because it doesn't try. It's rooted in coherence — when your thoughts, emotions, and actions align so cleanly that your energy moves as one. The authentic man doesn't need to chase attention because his integrity *creates* attention. People feel safe in his presence, even if they can't explain why.

The charming man mirrors emotion to fit in; the authentic man reflects truth to connect. Charm is like fireworks — bright, fast, exciting. Authenticity is fire — slow, warm, constant. One captures the eye; the other holds the heart.

In a world obsessed with impressions, authenticity is rebellion. Everyone is trying to be noticed, but few are brave enough to be *real*. The man who stands in quiet truth stands out effortlessly. His silence has weight. His words have texture. His eye contact feels like he's actually there — not thinking about what to say next, not performing understanding, just *present*.

That's the essence of charisma: full, unbroken presence. It's not about knowing what to say. It's about *being there when you say it*.

You can see it play out everywhere. The charming man tells a story to get a reaction; the authentic man tells it because it's true. The charming man laughs on cue; the authentic man laughs because something genuinely moved him. The difference isn't in behavior — it's in being. The charming man's attention is split between himself and others — he's constantly measuring his impact. The authentic man's attention is unified — all of it anchored in the moment.

That unity of focus is what people feel as charisma. It's what makes a woman's eyes linger longer, what makes friends open up more easily, what makes conversations flow instead of force. When you are fully in your body, when your energy is unfragmented, your presence becomes undeniable.

But authenticity doesn't mean emotional detachment. It means emotional honesty. You can be grounded and still warm, confident and still playful. In fact, humor is one of the purest expressions of authenticity — because genuine humor lives in presence. It's impossible to be truly funny while overthinking. The most charismatic men are not comedians; they're *comfortable*. Their humor isn't scripted — it's spontaneous, responsive, alive.

When you're authentic, even silence becomes connection. You can sit across from a woman, say nothing, and she'll still feel your attention — the subtle awareness in your eyes, the ease in your body, the steady rhythm of your breath. You're not waiting for your turn to speak; you're there, with her. And in that stillness, something rare happens: she relaxes. She feels safe. Because most people listen to reply, not to receive. The authentic man receives. He doesn't rush to fill space — he lets the moment breathe.

That's what creates depth. Depth isn't found in intellectual conversation or poetic words — it's found in how deeply you listen, how comfortably you hold silence, how fully you occupy the space between words. A man who can listen without losing himself, who can tease with warmth instead of insecurity, who can look without needing — that man creates connection without trying.

Presence itself is seductive. When you are fully here, she can finally stop performing. She senses that your attention doesn't wander, that your energy isn't desperate. You're not seeking something from her — you're *with* her. And in that space, she feels seen, not evaluated. Desired, not used. Safe, not suffocated. That's what real charisma does: it allows others to feel more alive in your company.

Charisma isn't built through volume or tricks. It's built through comfort with truth — your truth, her truth, the truth of the moment. When you stop hiding behind charm and show up fully as yourself, your energy stabilizes. You stop chasing responses and start creating resonance. People sense when they're in the presence of someone who's *aligned*. They can feel when you're not pretending — when your humor, your curiosity, your silence all come from the same place: peace.

And that peace is what draws people closer. Because peace is rare.

The charming man makes others feel excited for a moment. The authentic man makes them feel safe and awake at once. One burns out quickly. The other leaves an imprint. The authentic man doesn't need to dominate the room, because he *anchors* it. His calm creates contrast. His focus creates warmth. His humor creates ease. His honesty creates depth.

When you embody authenticity, connection becomes simple. You don't need tactics. You don't need to impress. You don't need to chase. You just need to *show up — fully, honestly, completely.*

Because the most magnetic energy a man can ever possess is this: Presence without pretense. That's the difference between being liked and being *felt*.

Boundaries in Love

Love without boundaries isn't love — it's chaos disguised as passion.

The masculine heart was never meant to dissolve completely into another person. It was meant to *contain* connection — to give it form, rhythm, and direction. Boundaries are not barriers that keep love out; they're the structure that allows love to breathe without collapsing. Without them, even the deepest connection begins to erode under the weight of confusion, resentment, and imbalance.

A boundary is not a wall; it's a compass. It's how you say: *This is who I am, this is what I allow, and this is what I won't become just to be loved.* When a man lacks that clarity, he becomes reactive — bending to please, agreeing to avoid conflict, shrinking to stay wanted. Over time, that erosion of self doesn't just weaken attraction; it kills respect.

The truth is simple: you cannot be loved fully if you are not respected deeply. And respect is born from boundaries.

The modern man often confuses boundaries with control, as if saying no or asserting limits means closing himself off. But control comes from fear. Boundaries come from clarity. Control says, *I need to dominate so I won't get hurt.* Boundaries say, *I'll stay open, but not at the cost of my integrity.*

When you set boundaries, you're not pushing love away — you're teaching love how to meet you.

In relationships, the absence of boundaries leads to polarity collapse. The masculine becomes overly accommodating, and the feminine becomes restless. She loses the anchor that once made her feel safe. Her testing increases, not because she's cruel, but because she's searching for strength — she's trying to feel the container again. When she can't, attraction fades.

Boundaries restore that container. They are the invisible edges that define your emotional leadership. They tell her: *I can hold your emotion without absorbing it. I can hear your pain without losing myself in it. I can stay grounded even when the energy between us rises.* That steadiness is the essence of masculine containment.

Containment isn't suppression. It's space. It's the ability to remain calm while someone else burns. To feel her emotion — her tears, her chaos, her fear — and still breathe evenly. It's not that you don't feel it; it's that you don't let it control your direction. That calmness doesn't distance you — it deepens intimacy. Because she can finally trust that her storm won't break you.

The man who cannot hold boundaries will always oscillate between two extremes: control or collapse. He'll either tighten in fear — shutting down, withdrawing, manipulating to regain order — or he'll surrender completely to chaos, losing his edge, his presence, his authority. Both destroy polarity. True containment lives in the middle: open yet grounded, firm yet compassionate.

Emotional leadership means you go first — not in dominance, but in regulation. You decide the tone of the moment through your composure. If she yells, you stay steady. If she withdraws, you don't chase — you invite. If she tests, you don't retaliate — you reassure through stillness. This isn't about being passive; it's about mastery. Because when you control your nervous system, you control the energy of the relationship.

You'll know your boundaries are healthy when you can remain open without being overwhelmed. You can say no without guilt, hold space without resentment, and love without losing focus. Your attention becomes a gift, not a leash. Your energy becomes a sanctuary, not a battlefield.

Women don't test boundaries to break men — they test to see if you believe in your own frame. When she feels your strength, she relaxes. Her testing isn't a challenge to your authority; it's a search for safety. When she feels your calm, her chaos softens. When she feels your clarity, her confusion dissolves. When she feels your steadiness, her trust deepens.

That's how boundaries protect attraction — they preserve polarity. The masculine thrives on purpose; the feminine thrives on feeling. Boundaries create the bridge between the two. They allow her emotions to exist fully without consuming your direction. They let you love deeply without drowning in her depth.

And this extends beyond romantic connection. Boundaries are the silent language of self-respect in every part of life — with friends, family, work, and even yourself. When you say, *I will not tolerate disrespect, distraction, or dishonesty,* you align your outer world with your inner standards. You stop negotiating your peace. You stop trying to convince people of your worth. You simply live it.

That's why the man with clear boundaries feels so powerful. He doesn't shout about them — he embodies them. His energy says, *I know where I stand.* And because he knows where he stands, everyone else adjusts accordingly. The weak resent it. The strong respect it. The feminine relaxes into it.

To lead emotionally without control means to trust your own strength so completely that you don't need to prove it. You hold your center and invite her back to hers. You guide through rhythm, not restriction. You lead by being immovable, not immovable by being rigid. You let emotion flow around you like water around rock — and in that stillness, you lead without saying a word.

Because leadership in love isn't about steering her — it's about anchoring both of you. It's not about fixing emotion, but holding it until it softens. That's what true containment looks like: a man who can remain open in the face of intensity, grounded in the face of chaos, and loving in the face of resistance.

Boundaries don't limit love. They deepen it. Because love without edges spills.

But love with structure flows — endlessly, powerfully, beautifully contained.

Boundaries in Love

Love without boundaries isn't love — it's chaos disguised as passion.

The masculine heart was never meant to dissolve completely into another person. It was meant to *contain* connection — to give it form, rhythm, and direction. Boundaries are not barriers that keep love out; they're the structure that allows love to breathe without collapsing. Without them, even the deepest connection begins to erode under the weight of confusion, resentment, and imbalance.

A boundary is not a wall; it's a compass. It's how you say: *This is who I am, this is what I allow, and this is what I won't become just to be loved.* When a man lacks that clarity, he becomes reactive — bending to please, agreeing to avoid conflict, shrinking to stay wanted. Over time, that erosion of self doesn't just weaken attraction; it kills respect.

The truth is simple: you cannot be loved fully if you are not respected deeply. And respect is born from boundaries.

The modern man often confuses boundaries with control, as if saying no or asserting limits means closing himself off. But control comes from fear. Boundaries come from clarity. Control says, *I need to dominate so I won't get hurt.* Boundaries say, *I'll stay open, but not at the cost of my integrity.*

When you set boundaries, you're not pushing love away — you're teaching love how to meet you.

In relationships, the absence of boundaries leads to polarity collapse. The masculine becomes overly accommodating, and the feminine becomes restless. She loses the anchor that once made her feel safe. Her testing increases, not because she's cruel, but because she's searching for strength — she's trying to feel the container again. When she can't, attraction fades.

Boundaries restore that container. They are the invisible edges that define your emotional leadership. They tell her: *I can hold your emotion without absorbing it. I can hear your pain without losing myself in it. I can stay grounded even when the energy between us rises.* That steadiness is the essence of masculine containment.

Containment isn't suppression. It's space. It's the ability to remain calm while someone else burns. To feel her emotion — her tears, her chaos, her fear — and still breathe evenly. It's not that you don't feel it; it's that you don't let it control your direction. That calmness doesn't distance you — it deepens intimacy. Because she can finally trust that her storm won't break you.

The man who cannot hold boundaries will always oscillate between two extremes: control or collapse. He'll either tighten in fear — shutting down, withdrawing, manipulating to regain order — or he'll surrender completely to chaos, losing his edge, his presence, his authority. Both destroy polarity. True containment lives in the middle: open yet grounded, firm yet compassionate.

Emotional leadership means you go first — not in dominance, but in regulation. You decide the tone of the moment through your composure. If she yells, you stay steady. If she withdraws, you don't chase — you invite. If she tests, you don't retaliate — you reassure through stillness. This isn't about being passive; it's about mastery. Because when you control your nervous system, you control the energy of the relationship.

You'll know your boundaries are healthy when you can remain open without being overwhelmed. You can say no without guilt, hold space without resentment, and love without losing focus. Your attention becomes a gift, not a leash. Your energy becomes a sanctuary, not a battlefield.

Women don't test boundaries to break men — they test to see if you believe in your own frame. When she feels your strength, she relaxes. Her testing isn't a challenge to your authority; it's a search for safety. When she feels your calm, her chaos softens. When she feels your clarity, her confusion dissolves. When she feels your steadiness, her trust deepens.

That's how boundaries protect attraction — they preserve polarity. The masculine thrives on purpose; the feminine thrives on feeling. Boundaries create the bridge between the two. They allow her emotions to exist fully without consuming your direction. They let you love deeply without drowning in her depth.

And this extends beyond romantic connection. Boundaries are the silent language of self-respect in every part of life — with friends, family, work, and even yourself. When you say, *I will not tolerate disrespect, distraction, or dishonesty,* you align your outer world with your inner standards. You stop negotiating your peace. You stop trying to convince people of your worth. You simply live it.

That's why the man with clear boundaries feels so powerful. He doesn't shout about them — he embodies them. His energy says, *I know where I stand.* And because he knows where he stands, everyone else adjusts accordingly. The weak resent it. The strong respect it. The feminine relaxes into it.

To lead emotionally without control means to trust your own strength so completely that you don't need to prove it. You hold your center and invite her back to hers. You guide through rhythm, not restriction. You lead by being immovable, not immovable by being rigid. You let emotion flow around you like water around rock — and in that stillness, you lead without saying a word.

Because leadership in love isn't about steering her — it's about anchoring both of you. It's not about fixing emotion, but holding it until it softens. That's what true containment looks like: a man who can remain open in the face of intensity, grounded in the face of chaos, and loving in the face of resistance. Boundaries don't limit love. They deepen it.

The Art of Attraction in Practice

We live in an age where dating has become effortless — and that's exactly why it's empty. With a few taps, you can scroll through thousands of faces, filter by preference, and "connect" without ever leaving your couch. But beneath the illusion of abundance lies something hollow: *nobody feels anything real anymore.*

Dating apps and social media didn't just change how people meet; they changed how people think about connection. Attraction used to begin with presence — with a glance, a tone, a shared moment of real chemistry. Now it begins with curation — filters, algorithms, and highlight reels. Instead of feeling each other, we *browse* each other.

The result is a culture of perpetual distraction. Everyone is talking, but no one is connecting. Everyone is available, but no one is *present*. We've turned intimacy into content, attention into currency, and the search for love into a marketplace.

And yet, despite all this access, most men feel more uncertain and anxious than ever. They're exhausted from chasing, performing, or guessing what women want in a world that runs on noise and appearances. It's not because they're doing something wrong — it's because they've forgotten the only thing that ever worked: *presence.*

The truth is simple. Attraction doesn't live in abundance — it lives in attention. When everyone's available, no one feels special. When everything is easy, nothing feels valuable. What used to make attraction magnetic was the element of *effort* — two people choosing each other out of all possibilities, not because it was convenient, but because it *meant* something.

Today's dating culture has trained men to chase volume over value. But a high-value man doesn't chase — he filters. He doesn't swipe endlessly hoping for validation. He moves deliberately, choosing quality over quantity. He knows that his time and energy are the most valuable currencies he has, and he spends them with intention.

If you want to stand out in the modern dating landscape, don't compete in the noise — *step out of it*. While other men play the numbers game, you play the depth game. While they perform, you *observe*. While they chase, you *choose*.

When you use dating apps, use them consciously. Don't treat them like slot machines — treat them like introductions. Choose photos that reflect your reality, not a polished performance. Write something that sounds like *you*, not what you think women want to hear. Then close the app, and go live. The more your real life becomes interesting, the less your digital life needs to be.

Dating apps should never be your strategy — only your supplement. You still need to move through the world with openness. Because real chemistry doesn't come from matching profiles; it comes from aligned energy. The modern man must relearn the lost art of *meeting women in the wild* — the everyday encounters that make connection feel alive again.

Here's how: When you see a woman who catches your attention, don't overthink it. Don't calculate the perfect line. Just approach with calm curiosity. Speak as if you've already earned the right to be there — because you have. You're not interrupting her day; you're offering her a moment of presence in a world starved of it. That's rare. That's what women actually feel.

Be the man who brings intention back into interaction. When you ask a question, mean it. When you compliment her, do it with precision, not excess. "You have great energy," said slowly and sincerely, lands far deeper than rehearsed flattery. Modern women have heard every line — what they haven't felt is *authentic energy*.

Understand this: women are overwhelmed with options but starved of leadership. They meet men who talk too much, type too fast, and feel too scattered. So when you show up grounded — when your attention is still, your breath steady, your gaze unwavering — you stand out instantly. You become the calm in a storm of noise.

Being selective is not arrogance — it's self-respect. You don't swipe endlessly because you don't need to. You're not searching for anyone to fill the space in your life; you're looking for someone who matches its rhythm. You know your mission, your values, your energy. You're not desperate for connection — you're prepared for it.

That's the new edge: *discipline in desire*. In a world addicted to instant gratification, the man who moves slowly is the one who feels powerful. The one who doesn't rush for attention, but allows attraction to unfold naturally.

So stop playing the modern dating game by its rules. Create your own. Lead with presence. Filter with purpose. Connect with honesty.

Because while everyone else is swiping for validation, the grounded man is building something timeless — a connection that doesn't need algorithms to survive.

The Magnetic Approach

Most men approach women like they're trying to solve a puzzle. They analyze every move, search for the perfect line, and end up sounding exactly like every other man who's trying too hard. But attraction isn't a formula you perform — it's an energy you project.

Women don't respond to words first. They respond to *states*. Long before you open your mouth, she's already reading your body, your breath, your rhythm. Is he grounded? Is he in control of himself? Can I relax around him? Those questions are answered in the first few seconds — and they have nothing to do with what you say.

That's why presence always beats performance.

The magnetic man doesn't approach with tension in his body or a script in his head. He walks with awareness — steady, unhurried, relaxed shoulders, even breathing. When he spots a woman who draws his attention, he doesn't hesitate or psych himself out. He simply notices the pull, accepts it, and acts on it without overthinking.

You're not interrupting her day; you're offering her something rare — a moment of genuine connection in a world full of screens and noise. That alone makes you stand out.

When you approach, lead with *energy first, words second*. Your expression should say: *I'm centered. I'm curious. I'm comfortable here.* If you speak, keep it simple: "Hey, I had to say hi — you have great energy." The sentence doesn't matter; the *delivery* does. Say it slowly. Make eye contact. Smile lightly, not widely. Leave a half-second of silence afterward. Let the moment breathe.

That pause is powerful — it's where attraction starts to form.

Because the pause shows you're not rushing to fill space or control the outcome. It tells her you're comfortable with the unknown — and that comfort is magnetic.

If she's open, let curiosity guide you. Ask about what she's doing, how her day's going, or what brought her there. The content doesn't matter nearly as much as the tone. You're not interrogating; you're exploring. You're making conversation feel like play, not pressure.

When she responds, listen with your full body — eyes, posture, stillness. Don't just wait to talk. Most men are thinking about their next move before she finishes her first sentence. The magnetic man listens in real time. He hears her words, senses her mood, and adjusts his rhythm naturally. That's how you "read energy" — not with tricks, but with attention.

You'll start noticing subtle cues:

- The way her tone lifts when she's engaged.
- The direction her feet point.
- How close she stands when you pause. Those cues tell you everything. Attraction isn't spoken; it's *felt*.

If she seems distant or distracted, don't force it. Detachment is power. Thank her for the moment, wish her a good day, and walk away with the same calm you arrived with. Because confidence isn't about always "winning" — it's about never needing to.

Approach isn't about getting a number or a date; it's about building your *presence muscle*. Every time you approach, you're practicing grounded communication — being seen, staying calm, holding tension without flinching. That practice translates to every area of life.

The more you do it, the more natural it feels. You'll stop seeing women as tests of confidence and start seeing them as mirrors of it. The energy you bring out there is the same energy you bring into your work, your purpose, your relationships.

Here's the truth: the men who attract women easily aren't necessarily the best looking or most charismatic. They're the ones who make women *feel something* simply by being in their presence — safety, curiosity, excitement. That feeling doesn't come from technique; it comes from alignment.

To meet women anywhere — the gym, a coffee shop, a crosswalk — remember this sequence:

1. **Notice.** Feel the pull of attraction without judgment.
2. **Decide.** Choose to act before your brain talks you out of it.
3. **Approach.** Lead with calm body language and genuine curiosity.
4. **Connect.** Listen, observe, and follow the rhythm of the moment.
5. **Detach.** Whether she's interested or not, walk away proud of your composure.

The real art isn't in what happens after she smiles — it's in how you show up before she does.

Because when you master presence, every environment becomes an opportunity for connection. You no longer need the perfect setting or timing. Your grounded energy *creates* the moment. And the irony is, the less you chase it, the more it finds you.

The Deep Connection Blueprint

Most men know how to talk. Few know how to connect. Conversation, for most, is performance — a rapid exchange of words meant to impress, entertain, or fill silence. But real connection doesn't live in constant sound. It lives in rhythm. In pauses. In the moments when you stop trying to be interesting and start being *interested*.

The truth is, women don't remember your jokes or your stories as much as they remember how they *felt* in your presence. Did she feel safe? Seen? Challenged? Excited? That emotional signature is what lingers. And it's built not through words alone, but through the balance between direction and awareness — between leading and listening.

Think of connection as a dance. If you try to control every move, it feels forced. If you refuse to lead, it falls apart. But when you lead with attunement — steady, intentional, yet responsive — the energy flows naturally.

When you first start talking to a woman, don't rush to prove chemistry. Start simple, but present. Instead of small talk that evaporates ("So, what do you do?"), ask questions that *breathe*:

- "What brings you here?"
- "You seem calm — what kind of things do that for you?"
- "What's something you wish more people understood about you?"

These questions work not because they're clever, but because they *invite emotion*. They turn the focus inward, giving her a chance to reveal, not perform. But here's the key: once she starts opening up, **don't hijack the moment.** Most men make this mistake — she shares something meaningful, and he instantly tries to match it, to relate, to one-up her vulnerability. That breaks the spell. Instead, stay with her story. Let the silence stretch a beat longer than feels comfortable. Nod. Breathe.

Absorb. Then respond softly, "That makes sense," or "I get why that matters to you."

That small restraint tells her everything she needs to know: *you can hold space*. You're not racing to fill emptiness. You're not afraid of emotion. And that calm containment — that subtle leadership — builds more trust than a dozen perfect sentences.

Leading in conversation doesn't mean dominating. It means guiding tone and pace. When she's nervous, slow the rhythm. When she's playful, match her energy without losing your frame. When she flirts, don't react too quickly — hold her gaze, smile slightly, and let her feel the tension. That's what creates emotional gravity. Tension and trust are not opposites — they're partners. Trust allows her to open; tension keeps her intrigued. The man who can build both becomes unforgettable.

The way you *listen* matters even more than what you say. Listen with your eyes, not just your ears. Watch how her shoulders relax when she feels heard, how her voice softens when she starts to trust the moment. Mirror her energy subtly — not as mimicry, but as resonance. When you adjust your tone to hers, when you breathe in sync, connection deepens beneath awareness.

And yet, don't lose your direction. If the moment drifts, bring it back. Ask something new. Tell a story that reveals who you are — not your achievements, but your perspective. A story that shows your humor, your focus, or your philosophy. Vulnerability, when expressed with composure, is deeply masculine.

Here's the formula most men never learn: **Curiosity builds comfort. Silence builds tension. Authenticity builds trust.** When you weave those together, you create emotional intimacy — the kind that draws her in without effort. As the night unfolds — or the conversation deepens — be aware of pacing. Connection isn't about saying everything at once. Leave things unsaid.

Let her wonder. Let her think about what you meant when you paused before your last sentence. Mystery isn't created by withholding information; it's created by *holding emotion.*

And when you're with her in person — especially on a date — your presence speaks louder than your words. Sit back. Breathe deeply. Speak slower than you think you should. When she laughs, touch her hand briefly, then pull back. When she tells a story, look directly into her eyes without reacting. These micro-moments are what make attraction physical.

What you're really doing is creating *emotional contrast*: light and dark, playful and serious, safety and spark. That's what turns ordinary conversation into chemistry.

The modern man loses women not because he lacks confidence, but because he lacks depth. He can talk for hours, but says nothing that moves her. He's predictable. Too polished. Too "nice." The grounded man, by contrast, keeps her leaning in — not because he plays games, but because every word feels intentional.

You don't have to be the funniest or most talkative man in the room. You just have to be *present.*

When you master this, connection stops being effortful. It becomes gravity. Women feel drawn to you not because of what you offer them, but because of how they feel when they're near you — relaxed, awake, alive.

That's the essence of deep communication: not performance, not seduction — alignment. You meet her where she is, and from that place, you lead her somewhere new.

Sustaining Desire

Most relationships don't die from betrayal — they die from stillness. Not the peaceful kind, but the stagnant kind. The kind where two people stop evolving and begin orbiting around comfort instead of curiosity. Attraction fades not because love disappears, but because polarity collapses. The early spark — that electric charge that once felt effortless — isn't meant to last by accident. It lasts when it's *fed*. And it's fed not by constant attention or effort, but by **the energy of becoming**.

In the beginning, desire thrives on mystery. You're discovering each other, testing rhythms, revealing layers. Over time, routine replaces that unpredictability, and many men mistake familiarity for intimacy. They start playing it safe, saying yes to everything, prioritizing harmony over heat. They forget that desire and comfort are opposites. Devotion without distance becomes suffocation. Distance without devotion becomes detachment. A relationship needs both — closeness to build trust, and space to keep curiosity alive.

That balance is the secret language of polarity. When you're too available, she stops reaching. When you disappear completely, she stops caring. The art is in moving between presence and absence with intention. Be fully there when you're together — attentive, aware, unhurried. But when you're apart, be truly *gone* — not checking in every hour, not seeking reassurance, but immersed in your mission.

Your absence should never feel like withdrawal; it should feel like direction.

The modern world teaches men to either overgive or disconnect entirely. Neither keeps attraction alive. What keeps a woman magnetized is your ability to stay in motion — emotionally, mentally, spiritually. When she sees that your world is expanding, her attraction expands with it. Because the deepest part of the feminine is drawn to evolution — to the man who keeps *becoming*.

Growth is the ultimate aphrodisiac. When she sees you training harder, speaking clearer, creating more, leading with conviction — she feels that power without needing to be told. She senses it in your tone, your eyes, the weight of your presence. It reignites something ancient in her: the desire to orbit a man who is in motion.

You don't have to make her jealous or play games. Just keep becoming a man she can't predict entirely — not because you're deceptive, but because you're alive. The predictable man is safe, but uninspiring. The grounded man is steady, but still evolving. That's the difference between comfort and chemistry.

Desire fades when polarity collapses. And polarity collapses when a man loses edge — when he stops saying "no," stops leading, stops challenging her emotionally and spiritually. The feminine craves movement, tension, and direction — not drama, but growth. If you can give her those, she'll never stop feeling drawn to you.

Keep dating her even after she's yours. Flirt in the kitchen. Whisper something risky when she least expects it. Surprise her with calm confidence, not over-the-top gestures. Desire doesn't live in routine; it lives in *presence reimagined.*

But remember — you can't sustain attraction externally if you've gone numb internally. Your own growth fuels the polarity. Every time you stretch yourself, you stretch the relationship. Every time you face discomfort instead of avoiding it, you bring fresh fire into her orbit. When you become more of yourself, she feels safer expanding into more of herself.

That's the essence of long-term desire: not control, not performance, but *co-evolution.* You both rise because neither of you is standing still. The most powerful relationships aren't those without tension. They're the ones where tension is *conscious* — where both people know how to move between closeness and independence, passion and peace, familiarity and mystery.

You don't sustain desire by holding onto it. You sustain it by staying alive inside your own mission.

Because the moment you start living for the relationship instead of from your purpose, she feels it. Your energy flattens. Your leadership fades. Your attraction weakens.

But when your mission remains your North Star — when she sees you driven, curious, disciplined, passionate — she feels that pull again, the one that started it all. Because women don't fall in love with a man's comfort; they fall in love with his direction.

So be her home when she needs safety — and her storm when she needs excitement. Be the stillness she can rest in, and the motion that reminds her what life feels like when it's alive.

You don't need to prove passion. You just need to *live it*.

When your presence deepens, your polarity sharpens. When your life expands, so does her attraction.

That's how you sustain desire — not by fighting time, but by feeding energy.

Because love is peace, but attraction is tension. Keep both alive, and you'll never lose either.

Become the Gravity

There comes a point when a man stops chasing what he already is. That's where your journey ends — and begins again.

You've walked through the noise, the conditioning, the performance. You've peeled back the layers of who you thought you needed to be. You've learned that attraction isn't built through tricks or postures, but through presence — that quiet, grounded force that says *"I'm here. I know who I am. And I move when I choose."*

Every man who reaches this place realizes something simple yet powerful: The goal was never to become someone else. It was to come home.

1. From Performance to Presence

The world told you to perform. To prove. To win attention.

That's what the entire "bad boy" myth was about — a misunderstanding of confidence as rebellion, when in truth, rebellion was just *freedom from the need to impress.*

The immature "bad boy" plays games to gain control. The grounded man no longer needs control; he has direction. He's no longer seeking the spotlight — he *is* the light. When he walks into a room, he's not asking for approval; he's scanning the world through calm awareness. His energy fills the space because it's *not trying to.*

That's the paradox you've now internalized: Presence begins the moment performance dies.

The world is filled with noise — men overcompensating for fear, women overwhelmed by imitation. The rarest quality left is stillness. When you embody it, you become unforgettable, because people feel safe in your gravity.

They sense that you won't bend with every social wind. You won't pretend for validation. You won't collapse when challenged. You're grounded — and in a world of floating, that's magnetic.

2. The New Masculine Ground

For too long, men were told that masculinity was either dominance or submission — tyrant or servant. But the modern masculine man transcends both. He leads *without control* and listens *without losing himself.*

He doesn't hide his intensity. He refines it. He doesn't suppress emotion. He integrates it. He doesn't seek equality through sameness. He honors polarity through respect.

And that's why modern attraction often fails — because everyone's trying to be everything at once. Men dim their energy to seem "safe." Women amplify theirs to feel seen. But polarity lives in truth, not politics. The masculine is direction; the feminine is flow. When you stand firm, you invite her to soften. When you're steady, she feels free to move.

This is not about hierarchy. It's about *harmony.*

The mature man no longer fears his masculine nature. He knows it's not aggression — it's presence, discipline, and clarity. It's the ability to hold space for chaos without collapsing into it. That's why your growth matters. Not to impress anyone, but to create the strength where love can actually relax.

3. The Inner Empire

If there's one truth that shaped every chapter before this, it's this: You are your own foundation.

Everything external — attraction, success, attention — is just a reflection of how you handle your internal world. When you lose that internal stillness, life becomes a series of reactions. When you own it, life bends around you.

That's why discipline mattered so much throughout this journey. Not as punishment, but as structure. Discipline isn't about control — it's about devotion. Devotion to your path, your peace, your power. A man who keeps promises to himself stops seeking permission from others.

You learned that the mind must serve you, not sabotage you. That the voice of doubt is only loud when you're still trying to convince yourself. That action kills fear, and truth quiets noise. You learned that strength and serenity are not opposites — they're partners. The warrior trains for impact; the monk trains for clarity. Together, they form the man who can fight without rage and love without fear. And ultimately, that's what mastery is: alignment between what you want, what you do, and who you are when no one is watching.

4. Dating in the Real World

Now that you understand yourself, dating becomes simple — not easy, but *clear*. You no longer chase women. You move through life *in direction*, and women feel that. You're not looking for validation through attention; you're looking for resonance through connection. The difference is subtle but seismic.

Modern dating is flooded with noise — apps, algorithms, abundance, confusion. Everyone's selling themselves like a brand. But that's why your calm, grounded energy stands out. You're not a product. You're a presence.

When you approach a woman now, it's not about saying the perfect thing. It's about reading energy — noticing how she feels, how you feel, and whether there's real curiosity. You meet people through your eyes, your tone, your body language. You let silence breathe. You listen not to reply, but to understand.

Every man who's mastered attraction knows this secret: *Women remember how you make them feel in your energy, not what you said.*

You don't need to impress; you need to express. Be genuinely curious. Be observant. Lead the conversation through energy, not performance. And when you feel a spark, don't rush it — direct it. Move with intention. Invite, don't chase. Show interest, not need. That's the art of the magnetic approach: your calm becomes her curiosity.

5. Connection and Depth

Surface attractions fade quickly. Depth endures. That's why connection — real, embodied connection — is the rarest form of seduction. Every deep connection follows a rhythm: tension, trust, and truth.

Tension keeps the polarity alive — it's the space between what's said and what's felt. It's the slow, unspoken dance of masculine and feminine energy.
Trust allows that tension to be safe. When she senses you won't lose yourself, she can finally drop her guard.
Truth creates intimacy — the moment both of you stop performing and start revealing.

When you speak from presence, you don't have to force intensity; it emerges. When you listen with stillness, she opens without needing to be convinced. You'll notice that the more grounded you become, the less effort connection takes. You'll stop asking "What do I say next?" and start asking "What's real right now?" Because what's real is always enough.

6. Sustaining Desire

The easy part is meeting a woman. The hard part is *keeping the energy alive*. Desire fades when growth stops. Love stagnates when comfort replaces curiosity. The secret is not endless novelty — it's continuous evolution. You stay attractive not by changing who you are, but by expanding your world.

Keep pursuing your mission. Keep feeding your fire. Bring that energy back into the relationship. When a man keeps growing, the polarity stays alive. His partner feels it. She may not articulate it, but she senses the difference between a man who *leads himself* and one who drifts. Desire isn't sustained by effort — it's sustained by expansion. You can't fake that kind of magnetism. You must earn it, daily, through discipline and depth. So, you don't "keep her interested." You keep *yourself alive*. And that, in turn, keeps the relationship alive.

7. The Legacy Mindset

Now, as you stand at the end of this path, one truth remains: Everything you've built means nothing if you don't embody it. Legacy is not what you leave behind. It's what moves through you while you're alive. It's the quiet example you set, the energy people feel when they're around you. It's the way your presence sharpens other men, calms women, and steadies the room.

You don't need to preach masculinity. You live it. You don't need to prove dominance. You express direction. You don't need to perform confidence. You *become* congruence. This is the new masculine code — not rigid, not soft, but *rooted*. Presence over posturing. Purpose over pleasure.
Stillness over noise.

You're no longer the man who reacts. You're the man who *decides*.

And because of that, your relationships transform. You attract from authenticity, not strategy. You love with power, not dependency. You lead by example, not control. That's legacy — to live in such alignment that your life becomes permission for others to rise.

8. The Return

Most men think becoming "magnetic" means adding something: more tactics, more style, more swagger. But true magnetism is subtraction — removing what's false, what's frantic, what's fearful.

You were born magnetic. Before the conditioning, before the algorithms, before the approval-chasing, you had natural direction. You knew when to move and when to wait. You trusted your instincts. You were clear. This journey wasn't about transformation. It was *remembrance*.

You've returned to that clarity — but this time, with consciousness. You're not naive anymore. You've faced the noise, the chaos, the doubt — and chosen silence, strength, and focus. Now, when you walk into a room, people feel it — not because you're loud, but because you're *anchored*. You've become gravity itself. You don't chase orbit; you create it.

9. Practical Reflection — Living the Code

Let's ground this final chapter in reality — what it means to *live this way daily*.

- **Wake up with direction.** Every morning, decide your mission. Even a small one. A man without direction leaks energy into distraction.
- **Master your inputs.** Limit the digital noise. Curate your attention as if it's sacred — because it is.
- **Train your body.** Strength breeds stillness. When your body is disciplined, your mind follows.
- **Honor silence.** Don't fill every moment with sound. Let boredom sharpen your instincts again.
- **Lead interactions.** Whether it's business, friendship, or romance, take initiative. Lead with calm energy, not force.
- **Stay curious.** Ask deeper questions. Most men listen to reply; few listen to understand.

- **Protect your standards.** Never trade your truth for temporary approval.
- **Keep evolving.** The journey doesn't end here — it begins anew every day you choose depth over distraction.

This is how you live magnetically — not through tricks, but through *truth*.

Some Final Words: The Quiet Power

Attraction has never been about strategy; it's always been about state. Confidence isn't loud, it's quiet. Masculinity isn't dominance, it's direction. Love isn't need, it's presence. You don't have to declare, "I'm the man." You simply are.

As you carry this into the world, remember that women don't fall for words — they fall for the space a man creates. The world doesn't respect noise — it respects clarity. And your life won't change because you've read these pages; it will change because you *live* them, daily, in silence, in action, in truth.

So walk forward not as a seeker, but as a signal. You don't follow trends; you set tone. You don't react to life; you resonate with it. You've remembered who you are — not the boy chasing approval, not the man performing strength, but the quiet presence that everything else orbits around.

You are not here to impress; you are here to express. You are not here to chase; you are here to choose. From this moment forward, move differently — slower, stronger, clearer. Speak less, mean more. Let your silence carry weight. Let your direction shape the air around you.

The world doesn't need more noise. It needs more gravity. And now — you are it.

www.ingramcontent.com/pod-product-compliance
Lightning Source LLC
Chambersburg PA
CBHW070614170426
43200CB00012B/2691